Internet Travel and Holidays for the Older Generation

Other Books of Interest

*****

Internet Travel and Holidays for the Older Generation

Jim Gatenby

BERNARD BABANI (publishing) LTD
The Grampians
Shepherds Bush Rd
London W6 7NF
England

www.babanibooks.com

Please Note

Although every care has been taken with the production of this book to ensure that any projects, designs, modifications and/or programs, etc., contained herewith, operate in a correct and safe manner and also that any components specified are normally available in Great Britain, the Publishers and Author do not accept responsibility in any way for the failure (including fault in design) of any project, design, modification or program to work correctly or to cause damage to any equipment that it may be connected to or used in conjunction with, or in respect of any other damage or injury that may be so caused, nor do the Publishers accept responsibility in any way for the failure to obtain specified components.

Notice is also given that if equipment that is still under warranty is modified in any way or used or connected with home-built equipment then that warranty may be void.

First Published - July 2004

British Library Cataloguing in Publication Data:

A catalogue record for this book is available from the
British Library

ISBN 0 85934 606 4
Cover Design by Gregor Arthur
Printed and bound in Great Britain by Cox and Wyman Ltd

About this Book

There's never been a better time to travel, especially now that many people retire with lots of good years to look forward to - or in the words of one Internet site for older people, "The Best is Yet to Come".

The Internet has played a major role in the recent increase in travel, with an enormous choice of discounted fares covering every mode of travel by land, sea and air. There are holidays of every type such as relaxing by the sea, adventures, sightseeing and special interests such as art.

This book shows how the Internet can be used to help you find and make your ideal travel and holiday reservations on your home computer. The book starts off with a brief overview of the facilities available on the Internet, including booking flights, ferries, cruises, trains, etc., and accommodation. Internet Webcams give you a "real-time" or live picture of your chosen resort and you can check out your hotel, cottage or villa, etc., with a "virtual tour" or short video of the rooms and the surrounding district.

This book shows you how to navigate the Web to find, extract and save travel information. Later chapters show in more detail how the Internet can be used for all of your travel and holiday arrangements, with a vast choice of special offers and last minute deals, such as flights to Ireland for only 99p - often exclusive to Internet users.

A separate chapter describes Web sites giving information on passports and visas, insurance, medical advice, holiday checklists, overseas embassies and consumer protection. The final chapter sets out to reassure the reader on the safety and security of paying for travel and holidays over the Internet and describes the steps you can take to protect your computer from viruses and Internet "hackers".

Travel and holiday Web sites of particular interest to older travellers (and also those with special needs) are included throughout this book and are also listed in the appendix.

About the Author

Jim Gatenby trained as a Chartered Mechanical Engineer and initially worked at Rolls-Royce Ltd using computers in the analysis of jet engine performance. He obtained a Master of Philosophy degree in Mathematical Education by research at Loughborough University of Technology and taught mathematics and computing to 'A' Level for many years. His most recent posts included Head of Computer Studies and Information Technology Coordinator. During this time he has written many books in the fields of educational computing and Microsoft Windows.

The author has considerable experience of teaching students of all ages, in school and in adult education. For several years he successfully taught the well-established CLAIT course and also GCSE Computing and Information Technology. The author is himself a member of what might loosely be called "the over 50s travel club".

Trademarks

Acknowledgements

The author and publishers would like to thank the following businesses and organizations for allowing extracts from their Web sites to be published in this book:

ABTA (The Association of British Travel Agents), Access Travel, ALL GO HERE, Arblaster and Clarke Wine Tours, ATOC (The Association of Train Operating Companies), ATOL (Air Travel Organisers' Licensing), British Airports Authority (Heathrow), Canvas Holidays Ltd, CenNet, Cheapflights Ltd, Classic Cottages Ltd, Contours Walking Holidays, easyJet.com, Ebookers UK Group, Eurotunnel, Ffestiniog Railway Company, Foreign & Commonwealth Office, F-Secure Corporation, Google Inc., Hadrian's Wall Tourism Partnership, Heritage Great Britain plc, In Venice Hotels, In Venice Today, John Flanagan Coaches, Mark Smith (The Man in Seat Sixty-One), Motts Travel, MyTravel UK Ltd, National Express Ltd, NYMR (The North Yorkshire Moors Railway), Omega World Travel (Cruise.com), Online Travel Corporation plc (ferrybooker.com), P J WebWorks (Croeso Cynnes), P & O European Ferries (Irish Sea) Ltd, Railtrail Tours, Remindalists Ltd (Don't Forget Your Toothbrush.com), SeaView Network Ltd, Shearings Holidays Ltd, Sherpa Walking Holidays, Shopping.net, Skytrax Group (Airlinequality.com), Snowdon Mountain Railway, State51 (Travel Knowhere), Symantec Corporation (Norton AntiVirus), The AA Ltd, The Disabled Drivers Assocation, The Disabled Drivers Motor Club, The Headland Hotel (Newquay), The Tarbert Hotel (Penzance), TheTrainline, Thistleyhaugh (accommodation on a Northumberland working farm), Time Out Communications Ltd, Travel 55, Visa International, Visitus Travel Ltd, Wallace Arnold Coaches Ltd.

Viewing the Latest Web Pages

The Web sites included in this book are used as examples to illustrate the text and are current at the time of writing. However, Web pages may be amended or updated from time to time; for example to change prices or to include special offers.

Readers requiring factual information such as prices, timetables, special offers, etc., are advised to view the latest Web pages on the Internet. The addresses of the Web sites featured in this book are given throughout the text, for example:

www.mytravel.co.uk

Enter the appropriate address into the address bar of a browser such as Internet Explorer to view the latest version of the Web pages.

Contents

4

5

9

10

1

Introduction

Why Use the Internet for Travel and Holidays?

Arranging holidays and travel the old-fashioned way can be a time-consuming and frustrating process; sending off for brochures and waiting for them to arrive in the post; traipsing around travel agents and endlessly scanning newspapers, never quite finding what you want. Having eventually made a booking you might reach your destination, only to find the hotel is a huge disappointment or not even finished.

Many older people are nowadays taking more holidays than ever before, often to far-flung places in the world. Arranging these journeys can be a complicated business; the arrival of the home computer and the Internet can make a tremendous difference in terms of time and convenience.

Some older people are hesitant to get involved with the Internet, fearing it is too complicated to learn to use. This is a misconception; older people can use the Internet with ease and so gain access to an amazing and infinite library of information. Quite naturally, many people are concerned about Internet security, especially in relation to financial transactions. Inexpensive yet effective Internet security precautions are described in detail later in this book.

1   Introduction

Travel companies, hotels and guest houses, etc., have been quick to embrace the Internet. By displaying their holidays and services as "Web pages" on the Internet, anyone with a home computer can see them immediately, from the comfort of their own home. The Internet can be used for the following tasks relating to travel and holidays:

- Viewing a hotel or guest house, looking into the rooms, restaurant, menus, disabled access, etc.
- Finding out about the surrounding area and places of interest. Many resorts now have "Webcams" - strategically placed cameras relaying live pictures to prospective visitors anywhere in the world.
- Checking for vacancies then making bookings "online", receiving immediate confirmation.
- Looking up the latest travel arrangements, finding out about times, prices and special offers on flights, ferry crossings and train journeys, etc.
- Most companies now have a Web site, so you can compare travel and holiday prices at a glance to get the best deal, especially last-minute offers.
- The Internet has incredibly powerful tools for *searching* for information, discussed in detail shortly. These tools are easy to use but can retrieve information from anywhere in the world within a fraction of a second. So whatever type of holiday you are looking for, the Internet will deliver the information, literally at the touch of a button.

No other medium provides the range of information on holidays and travel; information such as latest prices and last-minute offers can be updated immediately on a Web page, unlike the traditional brochure.

Later chapters in this book will give specific details of how to find and display travel and holiday information on your computer screen. The next few pages, however, give a few examples of the ways the Internet can be used to make your holiday and travel arrangements easier and more successful.

Suppose you wanted to arrange a short city break to Venice for example. Simply type the word Venice into the computer and the Internet responds with a huge list of "Web sites", or pages of information made up of text and pictures. Clicking the entry for a site on the list opens up the site and displays the Web page, as shown in the following example.

© 2004 Time Out Group Ltd

1 Introduction

The previous holiday Web page has lots of *links* to other pages. Links are words or pictures on the screen which can be "clicked" with the mouse to display more information. The previous Web page includes links to other pages giving details of hotels, restaurants, car hire and flights.

Arranging Flights

Numerous Web sites such as **ebookers.com**, **Onlinetravel.com**, **MyTravel.com** and **Cheapflights.com** display a wide choice of flights to destinations around the world, as shown in the extract below from **ebookers.com**.

You can select **Flights** or a **Flight & Hotel** before entering your precise travel details, dates, times, number in party, preferred airport, etc., and proceeding to make a booking. Links down the right-hand side of the screen can be clicked to reveal further cheap flight offers.

Arranging Hotel Accommodation

If you want to arrange your own travel or holiday accommodation, Web sites such as **ebookers.com** give a choice of hotels in major cities all over the world. (There are also apartments, budget hotels and cottages in France, Ireland and the UK)

Select a country such as New Zealand, for example, and enter a city, such as Auckland. You can specify the number of people in your party, the travel dates and the minimum star rating of the hotel.

1 Introduction

Click the **Find Hotel** button shown on the previous page and after a few seconds a list of hotels in the chosen city is presented, as shown in the extract below.

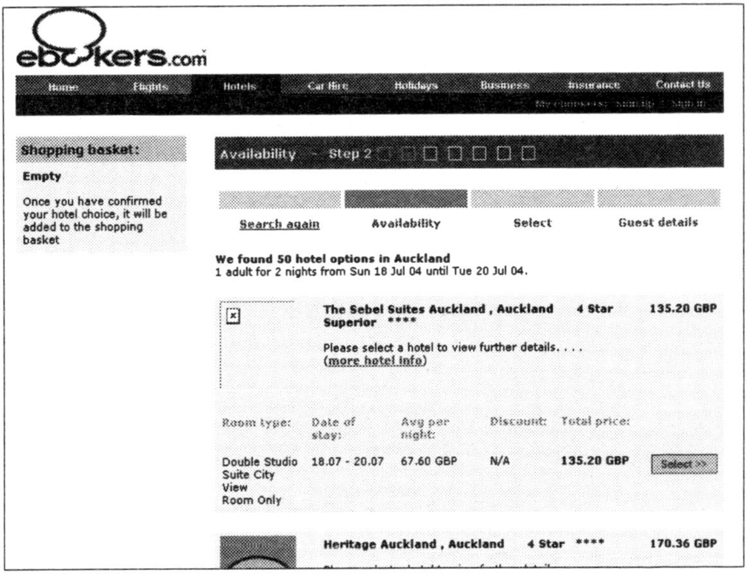

From the screen shown above you can look at the facilities of the hotels, (50 in this example), and check room availability and prices before making an online booking.

Please note that the **ebookers.com** Web site offers a complete range of travel and holiday services, such as **Flights**, **Hotels**, **Car Hire**, **Holidays** and **Insurance**, accessed by the menu bar across the top of the page, shown below.

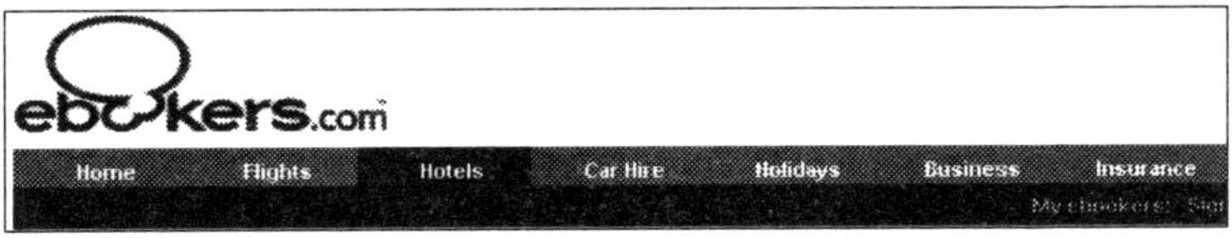

You can get a good idea of the inside of the hotel from the hotel's Web site. For example, the Tarbert Hotel in Penzance, Cornwall displays pictures of their different types of bedroom, as shown below.

The Tarbert Hotel site also includes information about local places of interest, tariffs, an online booking system and sample menus, as shown in the extract below.

Pan-fried Sirloin Steak Garni
Baked Chicken Breast stuffed with Leeks, Orange and Bacon
Seared Ostrich steak marinated in Lemon, Garlic and Worcester Sauce
Roast rack of Cornish Lamb accompanied by a Redcurrant, Sherry and Mint Sauce
Roast Monkfish with a White Wine, Saffron and Chive Sauce
Whole Baked Lemon Sole with Citrus Butter
Roast Sea-bass accompanied by a Lemon and Fennel Sauce

This sort of information on a Web page can be changed i.e. updated on a daily basis, if necessary.

Finding a Holiday Cottage

The Internet makes it easier and quicker to find a cottage to rent for a holiday. Web sites such as **Classic Cottages** allow you to enter all of your requirements, such as dates, numbers in your party, location, type of property, open fires, suitability for disabled people, etc. The Web site responds with lists of cottages matching the requirements you have entered.

Detailed maps are displayed on the screen showing the exact location of the cottage. Clicking on a particular cottage in the list displays full details of the cottage including one or more photographs.

If you like the look of a particular cottage, a single click will bring up an availability table, showing the weeks when the cottage is available or booked, etc.

From here you can complete an online option form as the first step in making a booking.

1 Introduction

Researching Your Holiday Destination

The Internet is an excellent medium for researching your next holiday destination. For example, if you were visiting Venice, you could find out a wealth of free information, using the Internet from the comfort of your own home.

The Web site **invenice.today** is a fine example, with over 300 pages of information about hotels, restaurants, churches, museums and exhibitions, etc., and there are maps to show the visitor the exact locations of places of interest. There are also links to hotels in the famous cities of Florence, Venice, Naples and Rome.

www.invenicetoday.com

Also see: **www.invenicehotels.com**

© In Venice Today 1999-2004

The In Venice Today Web site shown on the previous page has a link to a **PHOTO TOUR**. This includes maps and photographs of many of the amazing sights and fine old buildings in Venice, such as the churches, bridges and art schools. If you click **PHOTO TOUR** and then select **Churches**, a map and a list of the 7 main areas of Venice appears including San Polo, San Marco, Dorsoduro, etc. The location of each of the districts of Venice is shown by its number on the map.

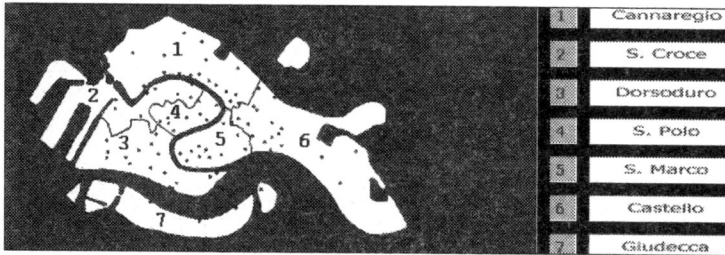

1	Cannaregio
2	S. Croce
3	Dorsoduro
4	S. Polo
5	S. Marco
6	Castello
7	Giudecca

If you now click one of the areas in the list shown on the right above, a separate map of the area appears showing all of the churches in that district of Venice. The screenshot below shows the **CANAREGIO** district with the names of the churches listed down the right-hand side.

SESTIERE OF CANAREGIO

1 S. MARIA DI NAZARETH (Scalzi) - XVII SEC.
2 S. GIOBBE - XV SEC.
3 S. GEREMIA - antica fondazione/ancient
4 GHETTO
5 SS. ERMAGORA E FORTUNATO (S. Marcuola) - IX-X SEC.
6 S. MADDALENA - XVIII SEC.
7 S. FOSCA - X SEC.
8 S. ALVISE - XIV SEC.
9 S. MADONNA DELL'ORTO - XIV SEC.
10 S. FELICE - X SEC.
11 S. SOFIA
12 SS. APOSTOLI - IX SEC.
13 S. MARIA ASSUNTA (Gesuiti) - XVIII SEC.
14 S. CANCIANO - IX SEC.
15 S. GIOVANNI CRISOSTOMO - XI SEC.
16 S. MARIA DEI MIRACOLI (Miracoli) - XV SEC.
17 S. MARCILIANO (S. Marzilio) - eretta/built XII SEC.

1 Introduction

To view details of a particular church, click the name of the church in the list on the right-hand side of the screen, as shown on the previous page. For example, clicking **S.FOSCA** in the list brings up details of the **CHURCH OF SANTA FOSCA** shown below.

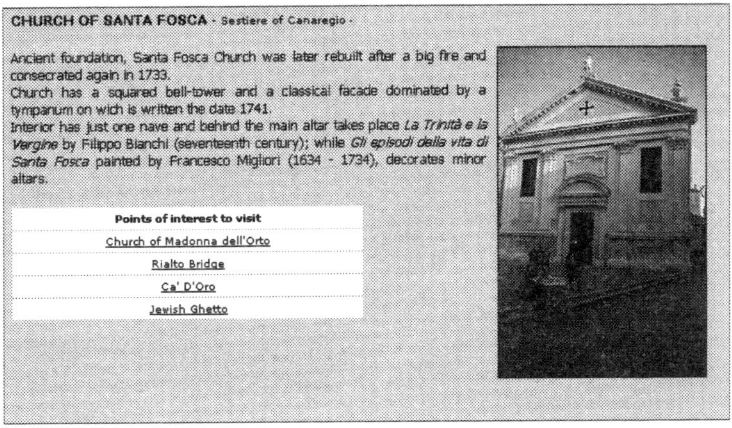

CHURCH OF SANTA FOSCA - Sestiere of Canaregio -

Ancient foundation, Santa Fosca Church was later rebuilt after a big fire and consecrated again in 1733.
Church has a squared bell-tower and a classical facade dominated by a tympanum on wich is written the date 1741.
Interior has just one nave and behind the main altar takes place *La Trinità e la Vergine* by Filippo Bianchi (seventeenth century); while *Gli episodi della vita di Santa Fosca* painted by Francesco Migliori (1634 - 1734), decorates minor altars.

Points of interest to visit

Church of Madonna dell'Orto

Rialto Bridge

Ca' D'Oro

Jewish Ghetto

A similar system of links presents photographs and background information on some of the bridges in Venice, such as the famous Rialto bridge shown below.

Webcams

Webcams are cameras permanently sited around the world in popular locations in major cities and resorts. Anyone with a computer connected to the Internet can view the pictures. Some of the pictures are live, so you can see people and vehicles moving; other Webcams take snapshots at intervals - every hour, for example.

The Fistral SurfCams in Cornwall, sponsored by the Headland Hotel in Newquay, were installed to show the current surf conditions to enthusiasts around the world.

While many older people may no longer be interested in surfing the waves, we can still benefit from "surfing" the Internet. Webcams provide all sorts of *current* information about a city or resort, such as the amount of traffic, the number of visitors and views of the surrounding area.

While a brochure or guide book may be several months old, information on a Webcam is completely up-to-date. Similarly, a well-maintained Internet web site can be updated with new information on a daily basis.

Getting Started

In order to use the Internet for planning and arranging your travel and holidays, you need a modern computer with a connection to the Internet via a telephone line. Any PC-type computer bought in the last few years will be adequate, preferably fitted with Microsoft Windows 98, Windows Me or Windows XP, the latest versions of the Microsoft Windows operating system. The operating system controls the menus or lists of tasks from which you make choices, by moving a pointer on the screen and clicking with a mouse.

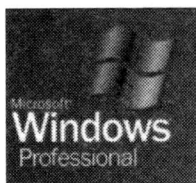

If you are completely new to computing, you might be interested in reading our very popular companion book, "Computing for the Older Generation" from Bernard Babani (publishing) Ltd. This explains the various parts of a computer and the process of setting it up and connecting to the Internet.

You might also be interested in reading "The Internet for the Older Generation" in the same series, which describes in detail the process of connecting to and using the Internet.

If you have not yet bought a computer, it's a good idea to find a small local computer business or enthusiast who will provide you with a machine for a few hundred pounds, including setting up the machine in your own home and connecting it to the Internet.

Finally be careful to protect your machine from viruses and "attack" from malicious Internet "hackers", trying to gain access to your computer via the Internet. Inexpensive methods of safeguarding your equipment are covered in Chapter 10, together with Internet financial security issues.

Displaying Travel and Holiday Pages

Introduction

The previous chapter showed some examples of travel and holiday pages displayed on a computer screen, using a program called a Web *browser*. Microsoft Windows, the software used to control the majority of desktop computers in the world, has its own built-in Web browser known as Internet Explorer. When you click the Windows **start** button you should see Internet Explorer as one of the menu options, as shown on the right below. Click on the **Internet Explorer** option to start the program and connect to the Internet.

If you are not familiar with a mouse, *clicking* refers to a single press of the left mouse button.

Double-clicking means two quick presses of the left mouse button. Double-clicking is often used to launch programs from their icons on the Windows Desktop, as shown on the next page.

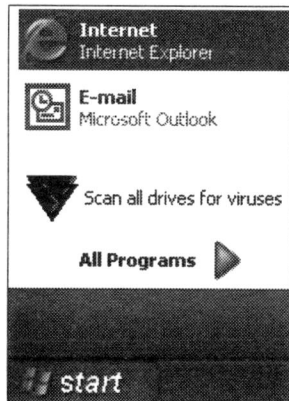

	Internet Internet Explorer
	E-mail Microsoft Outlook
	Scan all drives for viruses
	All Programs ▶
start	

The Desktop is the screen which appears after you first start your computer at the beginning of a session. Many of your programs appear as icons or small pictures, as in the Desktop extract on the right, which includes an icon for Internet Explorer. Simply double-click the icon to start the program.

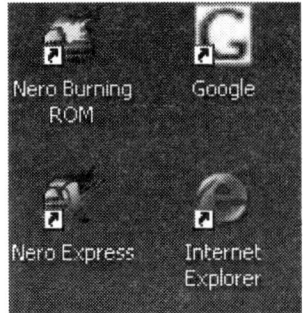

The next step is to make a connection to the Internet, via your Internet Service Provider.

Connecting Using a 56K Dial-Up Modem

If you are using a 56K modem, your computer should dial-up and connect to your Internet Service Provider.

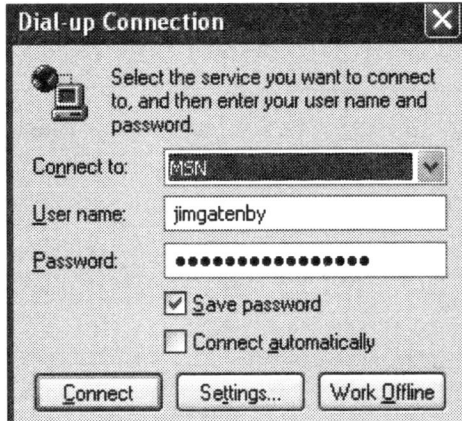

Your **User name** and **Password** are arranged with the Internet Service Provider after you sign up to use their service. Click in the box next to **Connect automatically** or click the **Connect** button shown above.

Work Offline shown in the previous **Dial-up Connection** window enables you to use the Web browser while not connected to the Internet. This will allow you, for example, to revisit previously viewed Web pages. When you browse the Web, some pages are saved on your own computer automatically. You can also choose to save Web pages for viewing offline, as discussed in Chapter 4 in the section on **Favorites**.

Connecting to the Internet Using Broadband

Connecting using broadband is a similar process, as shown in the DSL connection window below.

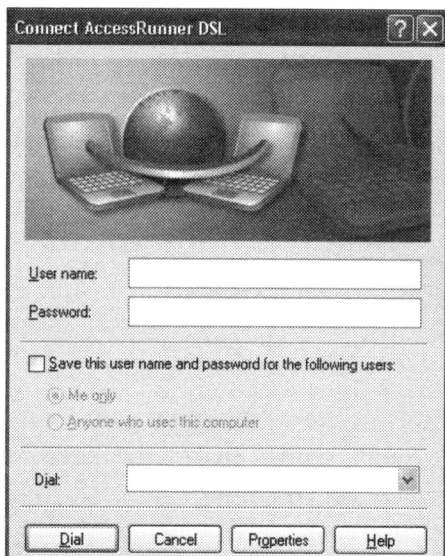

Once you have connected to a broadband service it normally remains online all day. (You pay a fixed monthly fee for broadband rather than being charged for the amount of time you actually use the service). Some broadband services don't require you to enter a password.

Your Home Page

When you start Internet Explorer it opens up and displays your home page. Shown below is the Microsoft UK home page, **msn.co.uk**. As described in the next chapter, you can choose to select a different Web page as your home page.

In the main body of the MSN home page shown above are various news items, with a list of the latest news stories. There is also a list of **MSN Channels**, giving information on a range of subjects such as the **Travel Channel** discussed shortly. A small extract from the list of **MSN Channels** is shown on the right.

The home page is the starting point for all of your Internet browsing. From here you can branch to other Web pages, using any of the following methods:

- Moving the mouse pointer and clicking over "clickable" links on the home page, usually pictures or special pieces of text, as discussed below.

- If you know the unique address of a Web page such as **www.travelandholidays.co.uk**, (a fictitious example), you can type it into the address bar at the top of Internet Explorer. On pressing the **Enter** key or clicking the **Go** button the Web site should be found and displayed.

- The browser also allows you to *search* for pages containing certain information by typing in *keywords*, such as **walking in Austria**, for example.

Clickable Links

As you move the cursor about a Web page you will notice that the pointer sometimes changes from an arrow to a hand. A piece of text may change colour and is also underlined, as shown on the MSN **Travel** channel on the right. Whenever the hand appears on the screen, this means the pointer is over a *clickable link* to another Web page.

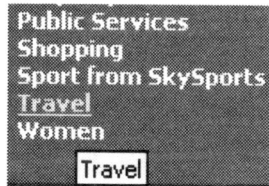

Pictures are also used as links to other Web pages, as shown on the **ebookers.com** Web site shown on the next page.

Each area on the world map shown on the right is a link. Clicking over an area such as **Australasia** brings up a list of holidays available on that continent, as shown in the extract below.

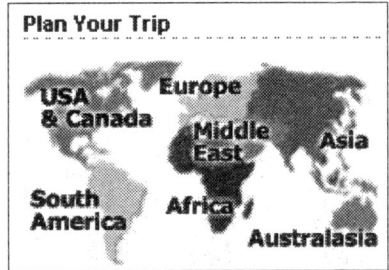

After you have followed a number of links and visited several Web pages, you may wish to navigate forwards or backwards through the pages. **Forward** and **Back** buttons are provided for this purpose on the Internet Explorer Toolbar, together with a **Home** button to return you directly to your home page, as shown below.

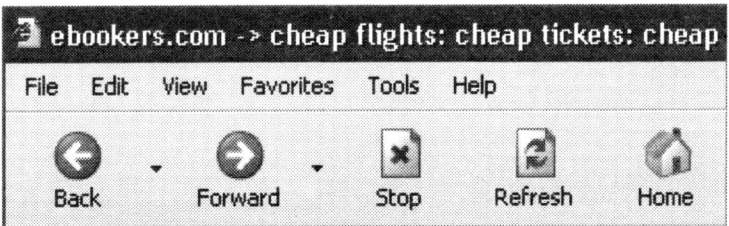

Entering the Address of a Travel Web Site

Every Web site has a unique address, such as:

http://www.travelandholidays.co.uk

The address can be typed into the **Address** bar of the Web browser, as shown below. To use this method of connecting to a Web site, you obviously need to obtain the address first, perhaps from an advertisement or newspaper article.

In computing jargon, the address of a Web site is known as a *URL* or *Uniform Resource Locator*. The meanings of the various parts of the address are as follows:

http:

HyperText Transfer Protocol. This is a set of rules used by Web servers. Another protocol used for transferring files across the Internet is known as **ftp**.

www

This means that the site is part of the World Wide Web.

travelandholidays.co.uk

This part of the address (fictitious in this example) is the *domain name* of the company or organization hosting the Web site on its server computer.

2   Displaying Travel and Holiday Web Pages

A domain name, such as **travelandholidays.co.uk**, is a unique method of identifying a company, organisation or individual on the Internet. After the main name, such as **travelandholidays**, various extensions are available, for example:

co   This denotes a Web site owned by a UK company

com   Company or commercial organisation

edu   Education

org   Non-profit making organization

gov   Government

net   Internet company

In addition, some Web addresses include the code for the country, such as **uk** as in the fictitious:

www.travelandholidays.co.uk

If you know the address of a Web site, enter this into the address bar at the top of the Web browser as shown below. (In practice you can miss out the **http://** part of the address.)

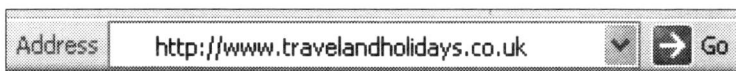

When you click the **Go** button shown above or press **Enter** your browser should connect to the Web site and display the required Web page on the screen. Then you can start moving about the site using the links within the page, as described earlier. If you click the downward pointing arrowhead to the left of the **Go** button shown above and on the right, a drop-down menu appears with a list of the addresses of your recently visited Web sites. If you click one of the addresses it will be placed in the **Address** bar and you can then connect to the Web site by clicking **Go**.

Keyword Searches

If you don't know the address of a particular Web page or you want to find information about a particular subject, you can carry out a *keyword search*. Suppose you want to find information about holidays for people interested in antiques. Enter the keywords **antiques** and **holidays** in the **Search the Web** bar in Internet Explorer, as shown below. Then click the **Search** button shown below on the right.

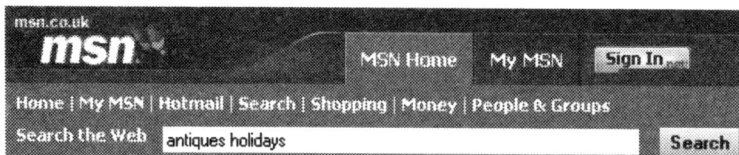

The results of the search are displayed almost instantaneously in the form of a list, as shown below.

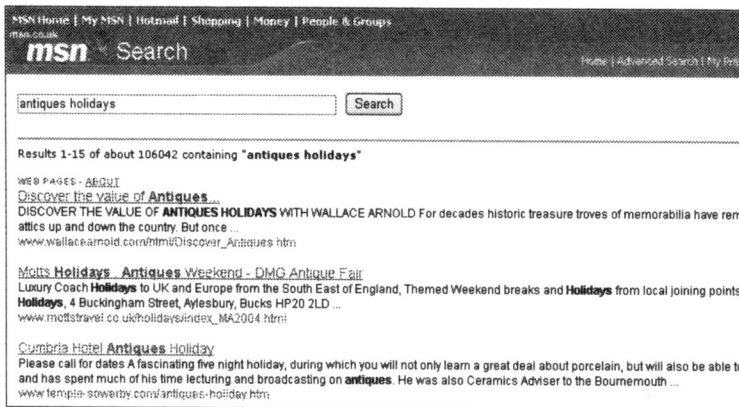

Searching Using the Address Bar

You can also start a search by typing the keywords into the **Address Bar**, as shown below, then clicking the **Go** button or pressing the **Enter** key.

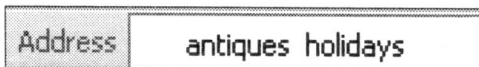

2   Displaying Travel and Holiday Web Pages

The results list on the previous page shows that the search has found a massive 106042 web pages containing the words **antiques** and **holidays**.

```
┌────────────────────────────────────────────────────────────────┐
│ antiques holidays                                │  Search  │   │
│                                                                  │
│ ┄┄┄┄┄┄┄┄┄┄┄┄┄┄┄┄┄┄┄┄┄┄┄┄┄┄┄┄┄┄┄┄┄┄┄┄┄┄┄┄┄┄┄┄┄┄┄┄┄┄┄┄┄┄┄┄┄┄┄┄┄┄┄│
│ Results 1-15 of about 106042 containing "antiques holidays"      │
│                                                                  │
│ WEB PAGES · ABOUT                                                │
│ Discover the value of Antiques...                                │
│ DISCOVER THE VALUE OF ANTIQUES HOLIDAYS WITH WALLACE ARNOL       │
└────────────────────────────────────────────────────────────────┘
```

Of course, the pages listed may not all be relevant to someone looking for a holiday involving antiques. For example, a Web page containing the words "A shop selling *antiques* is open on Bank *Holidays*" would meet the search criteria but is not relevant to this particular search.

Fortunately the search programs generally put the most relevant results at the beginning of the list of results. As discussed later in this book, there are also ways of narrowing down a search by including extra keywords, such as **antiques coach holidays**. This yields a relatively small 7477 results, compared with 106042 before the addition of the keyword **coach**.

```
┌────────────────────────────────────────────────────────────────┐
│ antiques  coach holidays                         │  Search  │   │
│                                                                  │
│ ┄┄┄┄┄┄┄┄┄┄┄┄┄┄┄┄┄┄┄┄┄┄┄┄┄┄┄┄┄┄┄┄┄┄┄┄┄┄┄┄┄┄┄┄┄┄┄┄┄┄┄┄┄┄┄┄┄┄┄┄┄┄┄│
│ Results 1-15 of about 7477 containing "antiques coach holidays"  │
│                                                                  │
│ WEB PAGES · ABOUT                                                │
│ Discover Holidays - Coach Tours To Cotswolds.                    │
│ Discover Holidays - Coach Tours To Cotswolds. ... com - Coach    │
│ Holidays and Tours at Discount P                                 │
│ at discounted prices ... B&B,Shopping,Art Galleries,Antiques,    │
│ Gifts Crafts,walking,Cotswold Way,C                              │
│ www.discover-holidays.co.uk/Coach-Tours-To-Cotswolds.html        │
│                                                                  │
│ Motts Holidays : Antiques Weekend - DMG Antique Fair             │
│ Luxury Coach Holidays to UK and Europe from the South East of    │
│ England, Themed Weekend break                                    │
│ points ... pitches offering a myriad of antiques and             │
│ collectables... ... Entrance to DMG Antiques fair                │
│ Street, ...                                                      │
│ www.mottstravel.co.uk/holidays/index_MA2004.html                 │
└────────────────────────────────────────────────────────────────┘
```

If we now look more closely at one of the results of the search, as shown below, we see that the first line of the result is underlined. When the mouse pointer is passed over this line of text, it changes to red, indicating that it is a clickable link to another Web page.

Motts **Holidays** : **Antiques** Weekend - DMG Antique Fair
Luxury **Coach Holidays** to UK and Europe from the South East of England, Themed Weekend and collectables........ Entrance to DMG **Antiques** fair. Motts **Holidays**, 4 Buckingham Street, ...
www.mottstravel.co.uk/holidays/index_MA2004.html

Clicking the top line above leads to the Web site of the travel company where there are more details of the holidays, the itinerary and the hotel and booking arrangements.

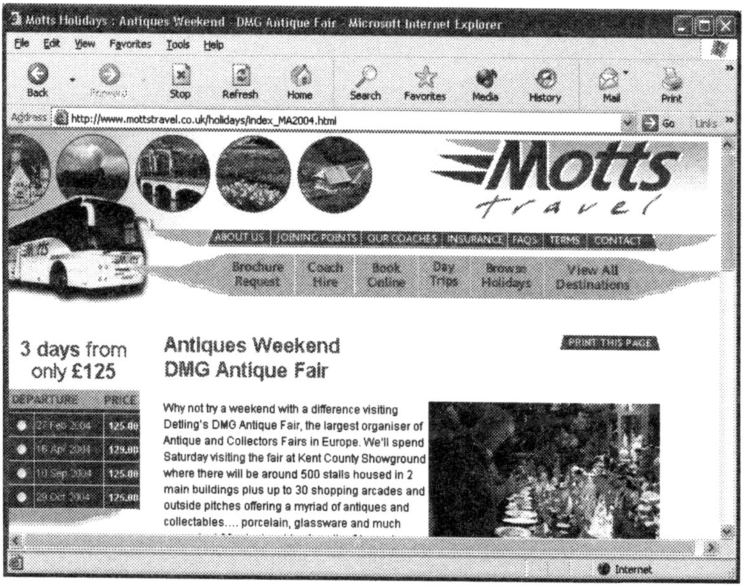

Another method of entering keywords in a search is to click the **Search** icon on the Internet Explorer Toolbar, shown on the right and in context on the Toolbar below.

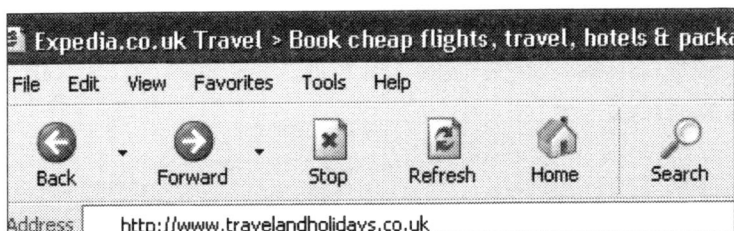

Clicking the **Search** icon opens up a **Search** panel on the left-hand side of the Internet Explorer screen.

As shown above, the search panel can be used to find a Web page as before, by entering the keywords in the box under **Find a Web page containing:**.

After clicking the **Search** button shown on the previous page, a list of search results is displayed as links, in the left-hand panel of the Internet Explorer, as shown below.

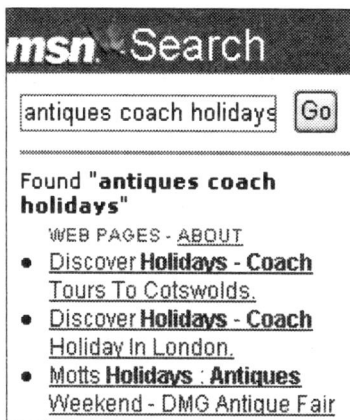

The right-hand panel displays miniature images of each Web site, as shown below. Clicking on any of the links above or the images shown below, opens the full-size Web page, with links to all the services of the travel company.

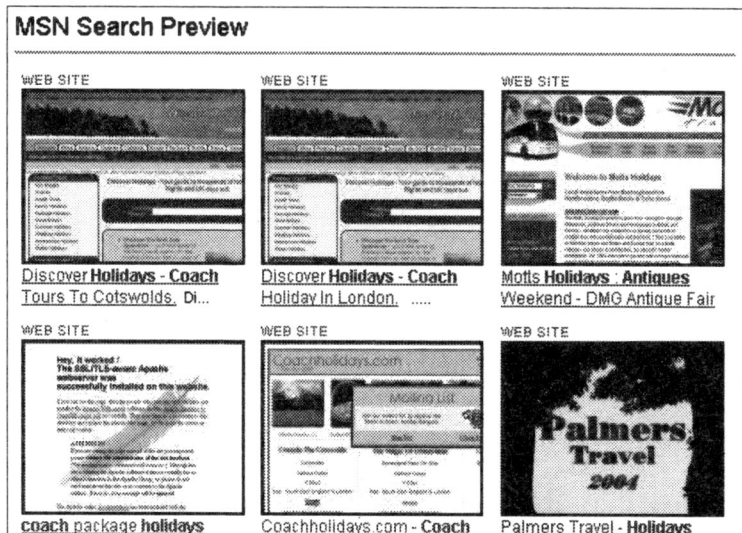

If you are feeling a little more adventurous, a similar search in MSN for **arctic cruises** produces the set of results shown below.

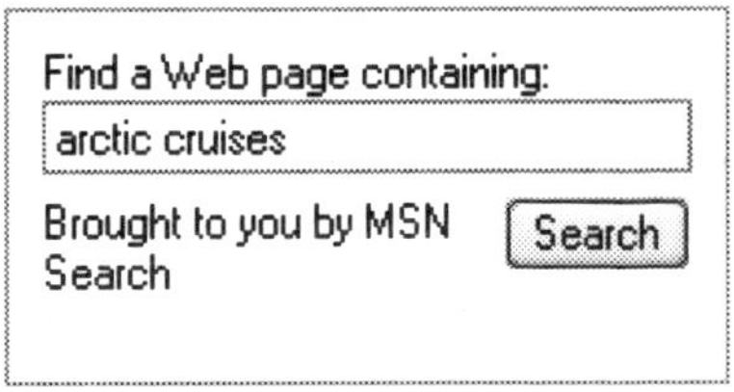

Find a Web page containing:

arctic cruises

Brought to you by MSN Search | Search

MSN Search Preview

SPONSORED SITE | SPONSORED SITE | SPONSORED SITE

Arctic Cruise Experts Let our **Arctic** Cruise experts help you find the per...

Your **Arctic** Cruise Experts Expeditions offers a variety of **Arctic cruises**...

Cruising Vacation in the **Arctic** Planning an adventure holiday in the Arti...

WEB SITE | WEB SITE | WEB SITE

Quark Expeditions, Antarctic **Cruises, Arctic cruises**

cruise vacation ar**ctic** Discounted cruise vacation **arctic** product or serv...

Birdfinders - Birdwatching Holidays - Antarctic and **Arctic** Cruises ... ...

Click on the small images shown above to display the Web sites of the various companies offering Arctic cruises.

Next

The next chapter introduces searching with Google, probably the most popular and versatile program for searching the Internet. If you can't find what you want on the Internet after searching with Google then it probably doesn't exist.

Searching for Travel and Holiday Information

Introduction

The last chapter showed how you could use the Internet Explorer to locate and display Web pages containing travel and holiday information. One of the methods described was the finding of Web pages by entering keywords into the **Search the Web** bar in the Internet Explorer. There are several other separate programs, known as *search engines*, designed specifically for searching for information from Web pages. Google is currently the most popular search engine and gives consistently good results; i.e. it rapidly finds Web pages which are highly relevant to your search and places them near the top of your list of results.

If you become familiar with using Google, you should be able to search the Internet for all your Travel and Holiday information, finding precisely what you want without a lot of irrelevant, unwanted results.

Google is free and can be launched by entering **www.google.co.uk** into the address bar of your Web browser, such as Internet Explorer, then pressing **Enter**.

Keywords are entered in the blank search bar in the centre of the screen, before clicking the **Google Search** button shown above. There are two *radio buttons*, shown above, allowing you to search the entire Web or alternatively confine the search to pages from the UK. A search may yield many thousands of results or none at all. However, if you think Google will find your site straightaway, click **I'm Feeling Lucky** as shown above. Then Google will immediately display the first Web page it finds.

For example, try typing **Channel Tunnel** into Google and clicking **I'm Feeling Lucky**. As shown on the next page, the Web site for Eurotunnel opens up straightaway.

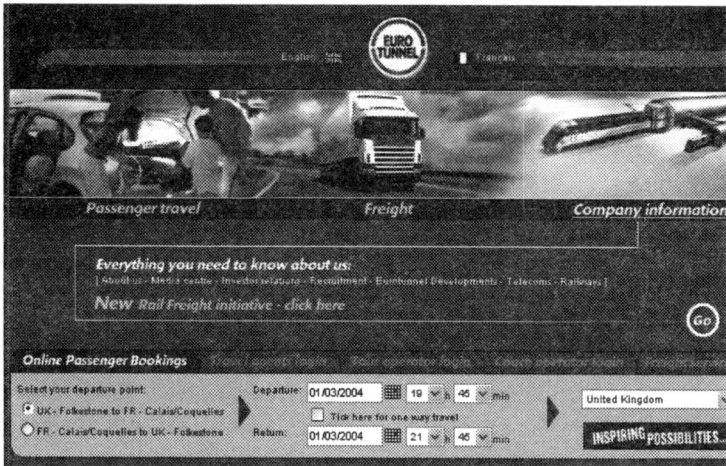

A search engine builds up a huge database by scanning all of the billions of Web pages on the Internet and taking a snapshot of each page. According to the screen shot on the previous page, Google was, at that time, searching 4,285,199,774 Web pages. These snapshots are placed in a store or *cache* where they are indexed. When you type in keywords, the search engine checks the cached pages and decides if the actual site is relevant to your search.

The list of results after a search consists of links to the latest versions of the Web pages, rather than to the original cached snapshots. As discussed shortly, the cached pages may not be as up-to-date as the very latest Web pages. However, Google allows you to view both the latest Web pages and the earlier cached snapshot versions. The cached pages can be very useful indeed, if for any reason the actual Web site cannot be launched.

Google is easy to use but there are a few simple rules which can make your searching even more effective. These are discussed in the next few pages.

Basic Methods of Searching with Google

Common Words

Google only includes a Web page in the list of results if the page contains *all of the keywords* in the query, except that common words such as **the, for, on**, etc., and single digits and single letters are generally ignored. So **Sutton on the Hill**, for example, would be treated as **Sutton Hill**. If you specifically want to include common words or single letters or digits, they should be preceded by a **+** sign, with a space before the **+**.

Capital and Lower Case Letters

You can enter your keywords in either upper or lower case letters. So **MEXICO, mexico, Mexico** or even **meXiCo** would all yield the same result.

Words in a Particular Order

If you want all of the keywords to be present on the Web page in a particular order, then enclose the phrase in inverted commas, as in **"Ashford in the Water"**. Otherwise Google will find all the Web pages containing the separate words **Ashford** and **Water** anywhere on the page.

We can check these basic rules out by searching for Sutton on the Hill, a small village in Derbyshire. If we simply type the basic name, **Sutton on the Hill**, into Google, as shown below, an unwieldy 247,000 results are returned.

The search results also stated that the very common words **on** and **the** were not included in the search. However, in this example we need those two words to be included. The search could therefore be modified to: **Sutton +on +the Hill** (include spaces before the **+** signs).

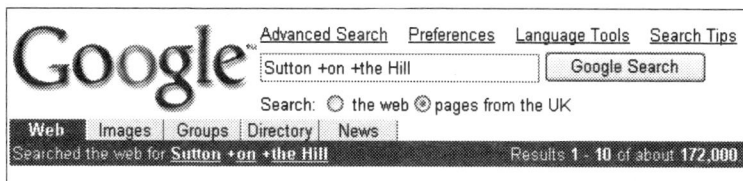

This has reduced the search results from 247,000 to 172,000, but there are still far too many irrelevant results. This is because the search engine finds Web pages where the words occur separately *anywhere on the page*, in any order. These separate occurrences of the keywords are shown highlighted in bold in the search result below.

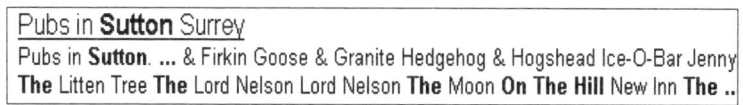

The Phrase Search

The way to eliminate this problem is to carry out a *phrase search*, by enclosing the keywords in quotation marks or inverted commas, as in "**Sutton on the Hill**".

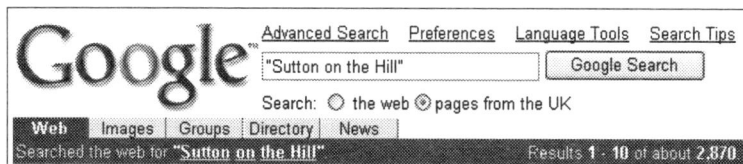

As can be seen in the previous screenshot, the search found only 2,870 results, all referring to the required village.

Eliminating Unwanted Results Using the Minus Sign

Many of the previous results included links to businesses in the area, which are not relevant to a search for Travel and Holiday information. For example, you wouldn't want to see links to dating agencies or double-glazing firms, which figure prominently in the list of results, as shown below.

Find Glazing Firms in **Sutton-on-the-Hill** UK - Double Glazing
You are here: Glazing > Derbyshire > **Sutton-on-the-Hill** We have found the following Glaziers in the town of **Sutton-on-the-Hill**: ...
www.point4glazing.co.uk/html/towns/ derbyshire-sutton-on-the-hill.html - 7k -

In fact Sutton on the Hill is a small village with no double-glazing businesses or dating agencies. These results are links to double-glazing firms and dating agencies all over the county of Derbyshire. The unwanted results can be eliminated by repeating the search after adding the keywords **dating** and **glazing**, preceded by the minus sign, as in **-dating** and **-glazing**, shown below. Remember to include a space before each minus sign.

"Sutton on the Hill" -dating - glazing   Google Search

Address   http://www.google.co.uk/search?hl=en&ie=UTF-8&oe=UTF-8&q=%22Sutton+on+the+Hill%22+-dating+-gl

Google

Advanced Search   Preferences   Language Tools   Search Tips
"Sutton on the Hill" -dating -glazing   Google Search
Search: ○ the web ◉ pages from the UK
Web | Images | Groups | Directory | News
Searched the web for **"Sutton on the Hill" -dating -glazing**   Results 1 - 10 of about 1,240

The inclusion of the minus signs and keywords to exclude Web pages containing dating agencies and double-glazing firms further reduced the results to 1,240 as shown above.

Narrowing Down a Search Further - Adding Keywords

A search can be narrowed down further by adding more keywords. For example, if we are interested in hotels near Sutton on the Hill. Adding the word **hotels** further reduces the number of results found to a more manageable 304 Web pages.

"Sutton on the Hill" hotels -dating - glazing   Google Search

---

Address http://www.google.co.uk/search?hl=en&ie=UTF-8&oe=UTF-8&q=%22Sutton+on+the+Hill%22hotels+-dat

Google™
Advanced Search   Preferences   Language Tools   Search Tips

"Sutton on the Hill"hotels -dating -gla: Google Search

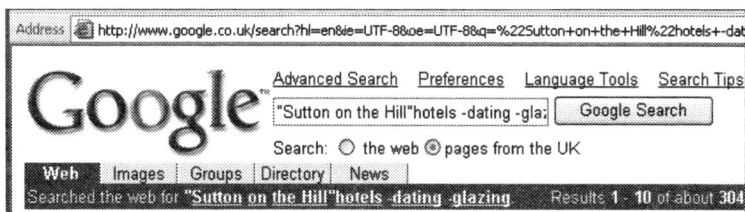

Search: ○ the web ◉ pages from the UK

Web | Images | Groups | Directory | News

Searched the web for **"Sutton on the Hill"hotels -dating -glazing**   Results **1 - 10** of about **304**

In this particular search, as the village is very small, hotels and accommodation are found in the surrounding area, rather than in the village itself.

Sutton on the Hill Hotels

Sutton on the Hill Hotel Booking From the Knowhere Guide

Looking for Hotels in Sutton on the Hill? Choose from our wide selection of Sutton on the Hill Hotels, check availibility and book online with our instant and convenient accommodation booking system.

Find a Hotel in Sutton on the Hill to suit every taste and budget, and search the surrounding area to find some great alternative places to stay nearby.

Hotels in Sutton on the Hill and Nearby

The Brookhouse Hotel Ltd - Rolleston - (2.6 miles) (map)

Single rooms from: £75.00, Double rooms from: £75.00

For more details click here.
To Book Online Click Here Now!

3   Searching for Travel and Holiday Information

The Web site shown on the previous page has links enabling you to book train tickets online or hire a car to reach your destination.

For other information about Sutton on the Hill from the Knowhere Guide, click here.

Get There By Train
Book Tickets Online! Click Here!

Hire A Car
Get Best Rates Now! Click Here

This Web page is provided by **Travel Knowhere**, (**http://travel.knowhere.co.uk**) and the site includes a database of hotels in the UK and France, with online booking, as shown below.

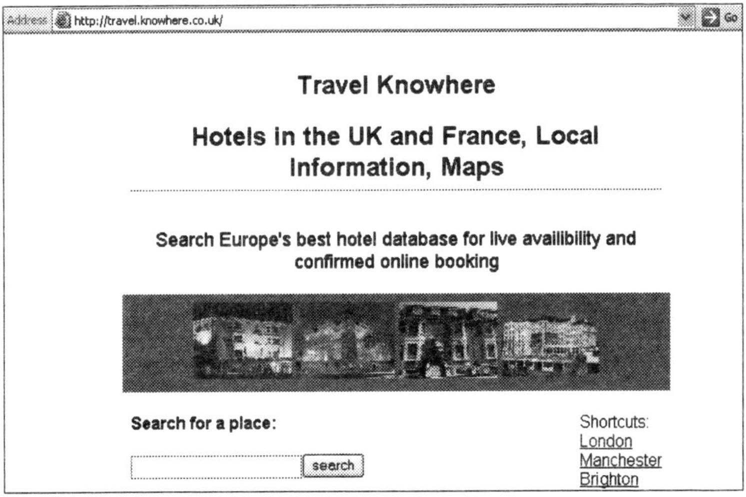

Address: http://travel.knowhere.co.uk/

Travel Knowhere

Hotels in the UK and France, Local Information, Maps

Search Europe's best hotel database for live availibility and confirmed online booking

Search for a place:

[   ] search

Shortcuts:
London
Manchester
Brighton

Using OR in Searches

Sometimes we may wish to consider two alternatives. For example, you might want to have a short city break and are undecided whether to go to Venice or Florence. You might enter the following search criteria into Google. Please note that **OR** must be in capital letters, otherwise it will be ignored.

| City Break Florence OR Venice | Google Search |

In this example, Web pages are included in the results if they include either **Florence** or **Venice** (and also the words **City** and **Break**).

Down the right-hand side above are links to major travel web sites such as Thomson, Leisure Direction and Expedia, allowing flights, hotels and cars to be booked online.

Search Results in Detail

Shown below is one of the results from the previous search for a city break in Florence or Venice.

Venice City Break at Shopping.net
You searched for **Venice City Break**. 1. **Venice city** breaks ... More Results
: [1] [2] [3] [4] ... **Venice City Break**. Shopping.net is a ...
www.shopping.net/venice%20city%20break.htm - 64k · Cached - Similar pages

   City Break In Florence at Shopping.net
   You searched for **City Break In Florence**. 1. **City** breaks ... More Results
   : [1] [2] [3] [4] ... **City Break In Florence**. Shopping.net is ...
   www.shopping.net/city%20break%20in%20florence.htm - 61k - Cached - Similar pages
[More results from www.shopping.net]

Google has found two Web pages on the same site which match the required search criteria, i.e. they both contain the words **City Break Florence OR Venice**. The link to the first Web page is the line **Venice City Break** at Shopping.net. The second Web page link, **City Break in Florence** at Shopping.net, is shown indented. Underneath each of the links shown underlined above are extracts from the text of each Web page. The keywords you type as search criteria into the search bar in Google are shown in the results in bold. Click the underlined link at the top of each result, such as **Venice City Break** at Shopping.net shown above. The Web page opens as shown below.

Cached Web Pages

At the bottom of some of the search results in Google the word **Cached** appears, as shown below.

City Break In Florence at Shopping.net
You searched for **City Break In Florence**. 1. **City** breaks ... More Results
: [1] [2] [3] [4] ... **City Break In Florence**. Shopping.net is ...
www.shopping.net/city%20break%20in%20florence.htm - 61k - Cached
[More results from www.shopping.net]

This is a very useful feature, as the cached Web pages are the original pages scanned and indexed by Google. They may not be identical to the current version of the Web page, but may still be relevant to your particular needs. Sometimes a Web page doesn't open when you click on its link at the top of a search result. The site may be temporarily unavailable or there may be some technical problem. In this case, the cached page provides a useful backup. Click on the word **Cached** shown above to open up the original cached page. Your keywords are highlighted in different colours, shown below as different shades.

You searched for City Break In Florence

1. City breaks in Florence
Book discounted scheduled and charter flights from all
the major airlines as well as holidays, **city** breaks,
hotels, attraction tickets, car rental and travel
insurance - Virgin Travelstore.
www.virgintravelstore.com

travelstore

---

2. City breaks in Florence from Deckchair.com
Founded by Sir Bob Geldof in 1999, Deckchair.com are
specialists in cheap weekend and **city** breaks to
Europe and the USA. Find your perfect **break** with our
build your own holiday tool.
http://www.deckchair.com

deckchair.com

Sample Travel and Holiday Searches

The next few pages are intended to show how Google can be used for specific searches for a wide variety of travel and holiday requirements. These illustrate the enormous volume of information on the Internet and also the power of Google to find relevant information quickly.

Finding a Cheap Flight

This example is for someone wishing to travel from London to New Zealand as economically as possible.

A vast number of links are found leading to airlines and agents competing for business.

Once connected to an airline or agent's Web site, you can enter your travel requirements, date, time, etc., check availability and make an online booking.

Finding Airport and Flight Information

Large airports throughout the world have an internationally recognized three-letter code. These can be found by a simple search in Google, as shown below.

Airport 3 letter code		Google Search

The extract below shows the 3-letter codes for the various London airports.

London	Canada	YXU
London	United Kingdom	LON
London - City Airport	United Kingdom	LCY
London - Gatwick	United Kingdom	LGW
London - Heathrow	United Kingdom	LHR
London - Luton	United Kingdom	LTN
London - Stansted	United Kingdom	STN

To find out latest information about flights, weather conditions, etc., simply type the 3-letter code, followed by the word **airport**. For example, Heathrow has code **LHR**.

LHR airport		Google Search

This leads to the Heathrow Web site, **www.baa.com**, which contains a wealth of information including flight arrivals, hotels, shopping and restaurants, etc.

Complete one or more of the options below to change the flight arrivals list:

Flight Number: Coming From: Terminal:

		All ▼

◐ **Click here to update**

Wednesday, 3 March 2004

Scheduled Time	Flight Number	Coming From	Status	Terminal
06.15	BI093	BANDAR VIA ABU DHABI	EXPECTED 1213	3
06.20	AA108	BOSTON	LANDED 0932	3
07.35	BA1473	GLASGOW		1
07.40	AA104	NEW YORK	LANDED 0824	3

Arranging a Ferry to Ireland

The following search may need refining later by entering possible departure points and destinations into Google.

Ferries Ireland		Google Search

This search produces a very large number of Web pages.

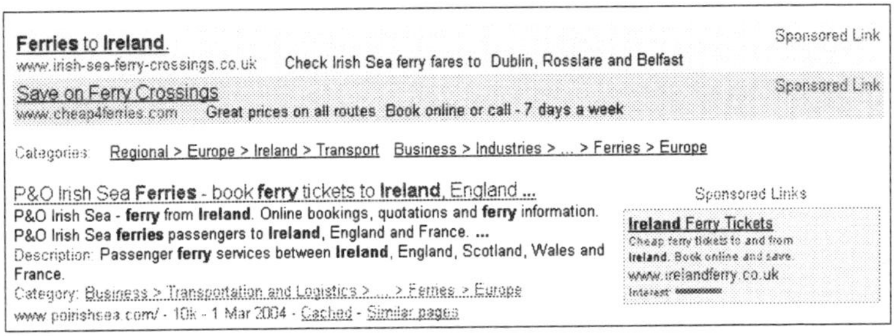

Clicking on the first result launches the home page of the **P&O Irish Sea** Web site, shown below. Click on one of the routes shown on the map below to obtain full details of the service and to make a booking.

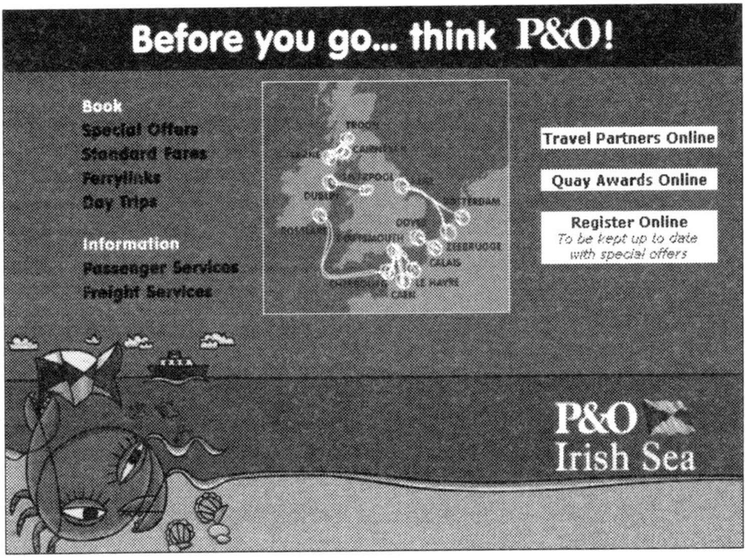

Finding a Coaching Holiday

With modern driving conditions, many older people prefer to travel by coach. Complete holidays, including excursions and couriers are often provided. Imagine you want to visit the Eden Project and The Lost Gardens of Heligan - a long drive from many parts of the United Kingdom. A suitable coach tour can easily be found as follows:

Coach Tours Heligan Eden Project	Google Search

As stated earlier, you don't need to include common words like "of" and "the" in your search keywords.

Web	Images	Groups	Directory	News

Searched the web for **Coach Tours Heligan Eden Project**. Results 1 - 10 of about 352

Coach Tours and Holidays to **Eden** & The Lost Gardens of **Heligan**
... **Heligan** with a guided **tour** of the gardens. DAY 3: Day **tour** to The **Eden Project**. DAY 4: Depart after breakfast for the homeward journey. Included in cost: **Coach** ...
www.angelaholidays.co.uk/eden_s2004.htm - 18k - Cached - Similar pages

Discover Holidays - **Coach Tours** To **Eden Project**.
... Discover Holidays - **Coach Tour** To **Eden Project**. <<GO TO www.discover-holidays.co.uk >>. **Coach Tours** and Holidays to **Eden** & The Lost Gardens of **Heligan** UK **Tour** ...
www.discover-holidays.co.uk/ Coach-Tours-To-Eden-Project.html - 31k - Cached - Similar pages

Sponsored Links

British Tours Ltd.
We cover this destination. Private tours of Britain since 1958.
www.britishtours.co.uk
Interest ▬▬▬▬▬

National Express
Top value coach tickets online from National Express - aff
www.nationalexpress.com
Interest ▬▬▬▬▬

Eden Project-Cornwall B&B
2 nights ensuite B&B & 2 fast track Eden Project tickets just £116 inc
www.rosehillcottage.co.uk
Interest ▬▬▬▬▬

You may need to refine this search further to find a coach tour which departs from your particular area.

Rail Tours

One of the most relaxing ways to travel is to take one of the many rail holidays now available. By entering the following simple search into Google, a huge list of links to rail holidays is displayed, in Europe and farther afield.

```
Rail holidays                        Google Search

 Web   Images  Groups  Directory  News
Searched the web for Rail holidays          Results 1 - 10 of about 632,00

Railtrail Tours: Main Menu
... cologne, werningerode, ayr, edinburgh, train, tour, vacation, scottish vacation,
scottish holiday, train tour, rail tour, rail holidays, holidays by train, uk ...
Description: Scenic and relaxing couriered holidays by train in the United Kingdom.
Category: Recreation > Travel > Specialty Travel > Rail
www.railtrail.co.uk/ - 13k - 1 Mar 2004 - Cached - Similar pages
```

These holidays combine sightseeing in spectacular scenery in countries such as Scotland, France and Switzerland with the sort of comfort only possible on a train journey.

RAILTRAIL TOURS LTD. Glencote Park, Station Road, Cheddleton, Nr. Leek, Staffs ST13 7EE
Telephone (01538) 361334 Fax: (01538) 361118 E-mail: enquiry@railtrail.co.uk

2004 Tour Calendar

Departs	Tour Title	Days	Tour Highlights
April			
Sat 24th	Le Lac et Le Mont	5	Paris, Annecy, Chamonix, Montenvers. - **FULLY BOOKED**
Fri 30th	Inspirational Gardens	4	Falmouth, Dawlish, Truro, National Museum of Gardening, Eden Project
May			
Fri 14th	Springtime Highlander	4	Glasgow, Fort William, Ben Nevis, Mallaig, Locha
Fri 14th	Orcadian Adventure*	4	Inverness, Dornoch, Dunrobin Castle, John O' Grc Orkney, Stromness
Fri 28th	Devon Steam Festival*	4	Plymouth, Tavistock, Buckfastleigh Butterfly Farr
Sat 29th	Romantic Highlander	5	Inverness, Brodie, Loch Ness, Kyle of Localsh
June			

This Web site informs us that the Eurostar train to Paris and beyond offers champagne lunches and full waiter service.

Special Interest Holidays

There are now holidays to match every conceivable interest including painting, cookery, whist, bridge, walking, bird watching and visiting stately homes and gardens, for example. Wine tasting in Burgundy is one holiday which might appeal to many older (and younger) people.

Clicking on the link at the top of the result leads to details of wine-tasting holidays all over the world, including walks through vineyards in Burgundy.

Sometimes a search result in Google will include a line of text starting with the word **Category**, as shown in the result below.

Arblaster and Clarke **Wine** Tours gourmet **wine tasting** tours to ...
... **WINE** TOURS to FRANCE **Wine tasting holidays** in the great French vineyards of Bordeaux, Rhone, **Burgundy**, Alsace, Provence and the Loire. ...
Description: UK-based agency with a large worldwide selection of tours and vineyard walks Includes tour descriptions...
Category: Recreation > Travel > Specialty Travel > Culinary > Wine
www.arblasterandclarke.com/ · 28k · 3 Mar 2004 - Cached - Similar pages

The underlined words to the right of **Category** are in fact a clickable link to the wine category in the Google *directory*.

Category: Recreation > Travel > Specialty Travel > Culinary > Wine

The Google directory is an alternative way of finding information. Instead of entering keywords into the search bar, you follow the categories down to find a particular subject. An extract from the Google wine category is shown below. In this example, the wine category contains a list of links to Web sites relevant to travel and wine. The Google Directory is discussed in more detail shortly.

Google Directory   [Google Search] Directory Help
                              ⦿ Search only in Wine ◯ Search the Web

Wine
  Recreation > Travel > Specialty Travel > Culinary > Wine   Go to Directory Home

Categories

  Guides and Directories (23)

Related Category:
  Recreation > Food > Drink > Wine (4207)

Web Pages   Viewing in Google PageRank order   View in alphabetical order
  California Wine Tours and Transportation - http://www.californiawinetours.com/
    Offers daily scheduled Napa Valley tours as well as custom tours of Sonoma and Napa valleys. Contains itineraries, fleet descriptions and rates.
  French Wine Explorers - http://www.wine-tours-france.com/
    Group and custom tours of all French wine-producing regions. Contains a schedule, profiles of the tour leaders, and useful links.
  Destination: Napa Valley Tours - http://www.tournapavalley.com/
    Creates winery, vineyard and historic tours in Napa Valley, California. Contains sample itinerary and menu.
  Wine and Dine Tours and Events - http://www.wineanddinetour.com/
    Personalized, escorted tours and corporate event services in Napa Valley and Italy. Describes offerings and gives

The great advantage of searching with Google is its flexibility - if you can make up a keyword search to match your requirements, Google will find the information if it exists. Here are a few more examples of productive searches. Remember that you don't need to bother with common words such as **in, the, on**, etc., unless it's an integral part of place name. In this case, enclose the complete name in inverted commas as in the following:

"Wells next the Sea"

In the following list of sample searches, all keywords have been entered in lower-case letters, although capital letters or even a mixture would achieve exactly the same results.

older people holidays ireland	Google Search
camping caravans provence disabled	Google Search
bird watching holidays norfolk	Google Search
castles northumbria -hotels	Google Search
walking mount kilimanjaro	Google Search
seniors holidays france	Google Search

In the **camping** example above, camp sites offering facilities for the disabled are included in the results by the addition of **disabled** as a keyword.

In the **castles** example, adverts for hotels have been eliminated by the addition of **-hotels**. Remember to put a space before the (-) sign.

The Travel Directory in Google

Previous pages have described the use of Google as a search engine, to find holiday and travel information by typing in keywords. Google has another very powerful approach to help you find relevant Web sites. This is the *Google Directory*, in which Web sites are organized into *categories*. Each main category is divided into further sub-categories, rather like the system of folders or sub-folders on your hard disc. To find Web pages on a particular topic you click on the category and sub-category headings until you find a list of sites meeting your requirements. To use the Google Web Directory, open up Google at **www.google.co.uk** and click the word **Directory** towards the top right of the screen. The Google Directory opens up as shown below.

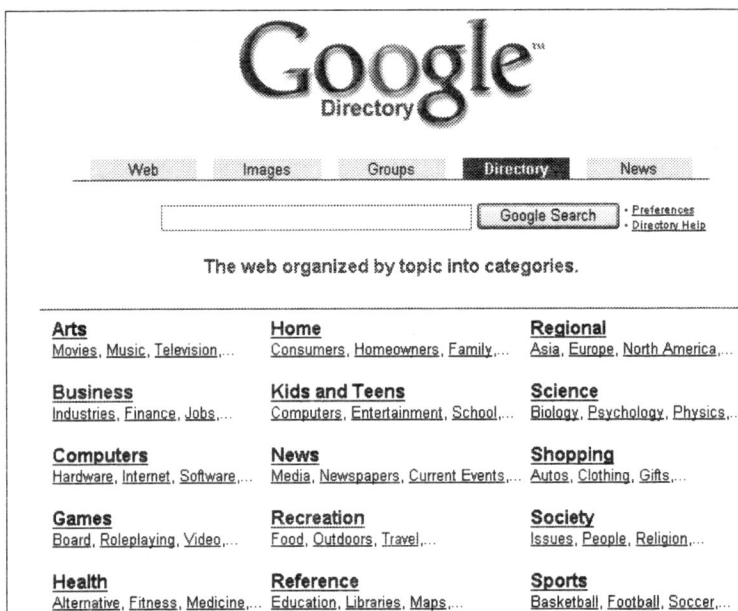

The web organized by topic into categories.

Arts	**Home**	**Regional**
Movies, Music, Television,...	Consumers, Homeowners, Family,...	Asia, Europe, North America,...
Business	**Kids and Teens**	**Science**
Industries, Finance, Jobs,...	Computers, Entertainment, School,...	Biology, Psychology, Physics,...
Computers	**News**	**Shopping**
Hardware, Internet, Software,...	Media, Newspapers, Current Events,...	Autos, Clothing, Gifts,...
Games	**Recreation**	**Society**
Board, Roleplaying, Video,...	Food, Outdoors, Travel,...	Issues, People, Religion,...
Health	**Reference**	**Sports**
Alternative, Fitness, Medicine,...	Education, Libraries, Maps,...	Basketball, Football, Soccer,...

Please note that although the Directory is divided into categories, the familiar Google search bar is still present. This can be used to carry out a keyword search *within a category*. The results of this search should be highly relevant since they are confined only to the required subject area. Referring to the previous screen shot, the **Travel** category is listed under **Recreation**. Clicking on **Travel** opens up the page shown below.

Travel
> Recreation > Travel

Categories

Attractions (34)	Lodging (547)	Tour Operators (11)
Consolidators (29)	Preparation (312)	Transportation (696)
Destinations (236)	Publications (225)	Travel Agents (21)
Guides and Directories (157)	**Specialty Travel** (3603)	**Travelogues** (1629)
Image Galleries (196)		

Related Categories:
Home > Consumer Information > Travel (36)
Regional (1539376)
Shopping > Travel (183)
Society > People > Expatriates (503)
Business > Hospitality (2177)

Web Pages   Viewing in Google PageRank order   View in alphabetical order

Lonely Planet - http://www.lonelyplanet.com/
Offers travel advice, detailed maps, travel news, popular message boards and health information. Also lists information and upda

Concierge.com - http://www.concierge.com
Information on popular destinations including essays from Fodor's, restaurant and hotel listings, maps, weather, recommended airfare finders.

AOL Anywhere - Travel Web Channel - http://webcenter.travel.aol.com/travel/airtravelhome.jsp
Includes destination guides, reservations, weather, and vacation information.

National Geographic Travel - http://www.nationalgeographic.com/travel/
Travel guides to US and Canadian destinations featuring worldwide destinations, maps and links to tools.

Frommers.com - http://www.frommers.com/
Comprehensive site lists extensive information on destinations around the globe. Includes activities, feature articles, guidebooks

The Virtual Tourist - http://www.vtourist.com
Interactive site aimed at learning from other travelers and sharing your travel knowledge. Includes chat, forums, travelogues, pho

At the top of the page, you can see that we are now in the **Recreation > Travel** category. Underneath are links to various sub-categories, such as **Destinations**, **Image Galleries** (maps and pictures from all over the world) and **Specialty Travel**. There are also links to **Related Categories**, such as **Travel** within the **Shopping** category. This category includes information about travel insurance and medical insurance.

At the bottom of the screenshot shown on the previous page are links to various travel companies offering a range of services

Web Pages	Viewing in Google PageRank order	View in alphabetical order

Lonely Planet - http://www.lonelyplanet.com/
Offers travel advice, detailed maps, travel news, popular message boards and health information. Also lists information and updates regarding their guidebooks.

Concierge.com - http://www.concierge.com
Information on popular destinations including essays from Fodor's, restaurant and hotel listings, maps, weather, recommended readings, currency rates and airfare finders.

AOL Anywhere - Travel Web Channel - http://webcenter.travel.aol.com/travel/air/travelhome.jsp
Includes destination guides, reservations, weather, and vacation information.

National Geographic Travel - http://www.nationalgeographic.com/travel/
Travel guides to US and Canadian destinations featuring worldwide destinations, maps and links to tools.

Frommers.com - http://www.frommers.com/
Comprehensive site lists extensive information on destinations around the globe. Includes activities, feature articles, guidebooks and message boards.

The Virtual Tourist - http://www.vtourist.com
Interactive site aimed at learning from other travelers and sharing your travel knowledge. Includes chat, forums, travelogues, photos and maps.

Fodor's Travel Online - http://www.fodors.com/
In-depth restaurant and hotel reviews in cities around the world, and smart travel tips to make vacation planning easier.

You can find out information on most aspects of travel. The **Lonely Planet** site includes, amongst other things, travel advice, message boards, maps, news and health information.

Lonely Planet - http://www.lonelyplanet.com/
Offers travel advice, detailed maps, travel news, popular and health information. Also lists information and upda

The **Virtual Tourist** site enables travellers to exchange experiences through an online "chat" facility.

The Virtual Tourist - http://www.vtourist.com
Interactive site aimed at learning from other travelers
Includes chat, forums, travelogues, photos and maps.

Within the list of **Travel** categories shown below, we might choose to have a look at **Specialty Travel**, for example.

Travel
Recreation > Travel

Categories

Attractions (34)
Consolidators (29)
Destinations (236)
Guides and Directories (157)
Image Galleries (196)

Lodging (847)
Preparation (312)
Publications (226)
Specialty Travel (3603)

Tour Operators (11)
Transportation (696)
Travel Agents (21)
Travelogues (1829)

Clicking the **Specialty Travel** link leads to the sub-category **Recreation > Travel > Specialty Travel** shown below.

Specialty Travel
Recreation > Travel > Specialty Travel

Categories

Adventure and Sports (301)
African American (19)
Archaeology (38)
Arts (109)
Backpacking (117)
Battlefields (22)
Boat Charters (900)
Budget (47)
Camping (3195)
Catholic (13)
Christian (49)
Corporate (192)
Cruises (537)
Culinary (150)
Disabled (306)
Ecotourism (390)

Educational (58)
Equestrian (723)
Family (67)
Festivals and Holidays (11)
Gaming Junkets (21)
Gay, Lesbian, and Bisexual (588)
Holistic (40)
Hospitality Clubs (20)
Jewish (60)
Mystery (9)
Native American (14)
Nudism (81)
Outdoors (18583)
Photography (110)
Pilgrimage (50)
Rail (38)

Science (26)
Scuba Diving (127)
Seniors (28)
Singles (21)
Smoke Free (3)
Space (5)
Spas (117)
Students (103)
Supernatural (31)
Theme Parks (808)
Vegetarianism (13)
Volunteering (39)
Weddings and Honeymoons (36)
With Pets (100)
Women (52)
Working Holidays (22)

As you can see, there is a huge choice of specialty travel Web pages, including boating, camping, culinary, disabled, photography, pets and supernatural.

3   Searching for Travel and Holiday Information

As an example, if we click **Disabled**, as shown on the previous page, the following list of categories appears.

Travel
Society > Disabled > Travel

Categories

Agencies (23)   Senior Travel (28)   Sports (359)
Airlines (13)   Seniors (11)   Wheelchair (4)
Cruises (5)   Specific   Wheelchair and Electric Scooter
Rental Vans and Hand- Disabilities (24)   Rentals (17)
Controls (19)   Specific Places (182)

The above list of categories shows there is a wealth of information for disabled travellers and also for **Senior Travel** and **Seniors**. Clicking on **Seniors** for example, produces the following Web sites for older travellers.

Seniors
Recreation > Travel > Specialty Travel > Seniors

Related Category.
Society > People > Seniors (1550)

Web Pages   Viewing in Google PageRank order   View in alphabet

Elderhostel - http://www.elderhostel.org/
Provides adventures for older adults through educational travel programs throughout the world.

ElderTreks - http://www.eldertreks.com
Adventure travel company for people 50 and over. Travel to over 50 exotic countries in small gr

50plus Expeditions - http://www.50plusExpeditions.com/
Adventure travel company specializing in trips for travelers 50 and over. Includes package desc
and contact details.

Snowbirdhelper.com - http://www.snowbirdhelper.com
Snowbirdhelper most complete travel tool for Snowbirds, Potential Snowbirds or warm weather
needed for travel. Maps, hotels, airline tickets, events, tourist information, weather, online store

Double Nickels - http://www.doublenickels.com/page3.html
Senior travel information

New Zealand Tours for Seniors - http://www.newzealandseniortravel.com/
Helping retired and semi-retired people enjoy New Zealand in comfortable, safe tours organized
resident couple.

Click on any of the links shown underlined above to find special holidays and travel opportunities for older people, including online booking arrangements.

4

Capturing Travel and Holiday Web Pages

The last chapter showed how you can search for and display travel and holiday Web pages. This chapter describes methods for "book marking" and returning to previously visited Web sites. Also described are methods of saving Web pages or parts of pages on your computer's hard disc.

If you find a really useful Web site, you might want to return again at a later date. Fortunately you don't need to repeat the process of searching for the site or typing in the Web address, etc. Internet Explorer includes two features for returning directly to a previously visited site. These are the **Favorites** feature and the **History** feature, launched by clicking their icons on the right of the Toolbar, shown below. You can also use the **Favorites** option on the menu bar shown below, next to **File, Edit** and **View**.

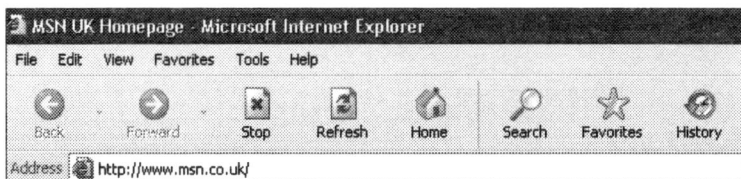

Revisiting Web Sites - The Favorites Feature

If you are displaying a Web site which may be useful in future, a link to the site can be saved or "bookmarked" after clicking the **Favorites** icon on the Toolbar in Internet Explorer.

After you select **Favorites**, a panel opens on the left of the screen, displaying a list of Web sites, as shown below left.

To place the current Web site on your list of **Favorites** click the **Add...** button shown above on the left. In this case I am adding **Sherpa Walking Holidays in Austria** to my list of **Favorites**. A dialogue box opens up as shown below.

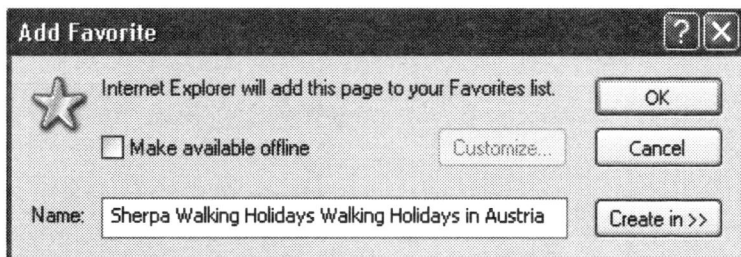

Note in the **Add Favorite** dialogue box shown below, you can insert a name of your own in the **Name** bar, if you wish. There is also a check box to tick if you want the Web pages to be viewable offline, i.e. without being connected to the Internet.

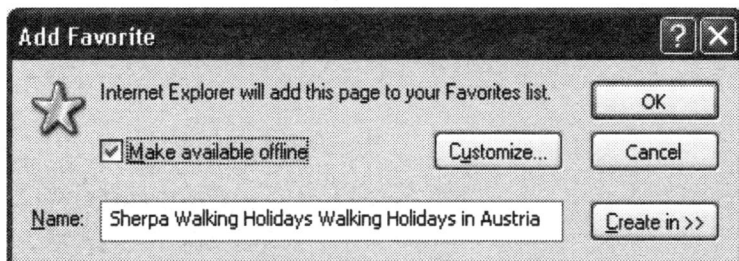

Clicking the **Customize...** button shown above allows you to decide how much of the Web site you want to make available for offline viewing. Finally click **OK** to add the site to your list of **Favorites**.

To return to the Web site at a later date, click the **Favorites** icon on the Internet Explorer Toolbar, then click the name of the Web site in the list, such as **Sherpa Walking Holidays**, shown below.

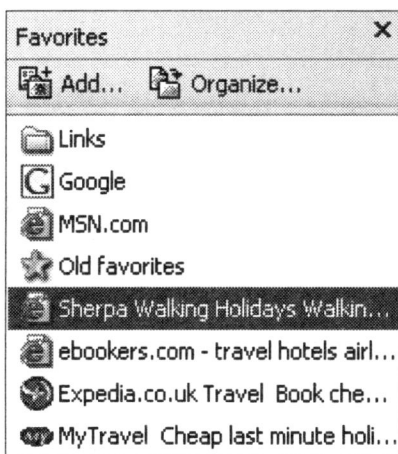

The Web site will open on the screen if it was previously saved for viewing offline. If the Web site is not available offline, the computer will connect to the Internet and display the required site.

As your browsing will probably involve a variety of Internet sites, it's a good idea to divide your **Favorites** into various categories or *folders*. Otherwise the list of **Favorites** can become very long and unmanageable.

To create a system of folders for your **Favorites**, click the **Organize...** button at the top of the **Favorites** panel, as shown in the extract on the right. The **Organize Favorites** window appears, as shown on the next page.

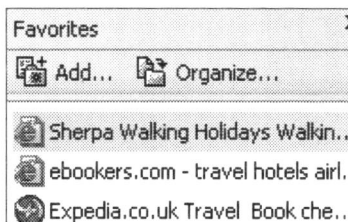

If you now click the **Create Folder** button, as shown below, a bar appears containing the words **New Folder**, which you replace with your own name for the new folder.

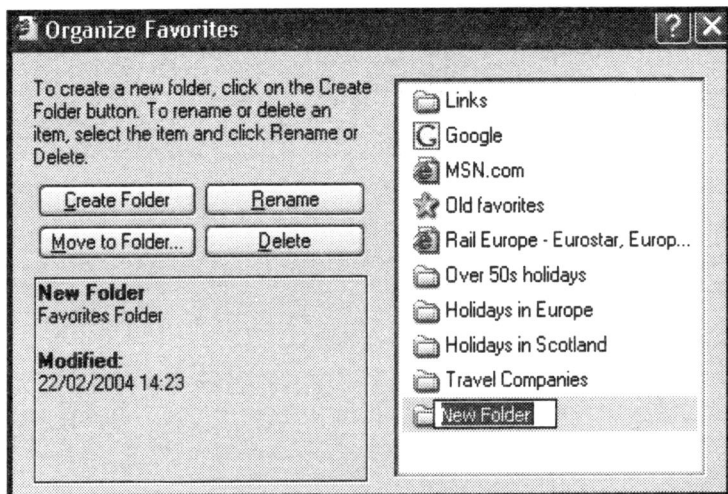

Now you can place your **Favorites** in the appropriate folders. This can be done by selecting the link in the right-hand panel shown above, then clicking the **Move to Folder...** button shown on the left above. Then select the destination folder from the **Browse for Folder** window which appears. In the example on the right, a group of **Favorites** has been organized into a folder called **Travel Companies**.

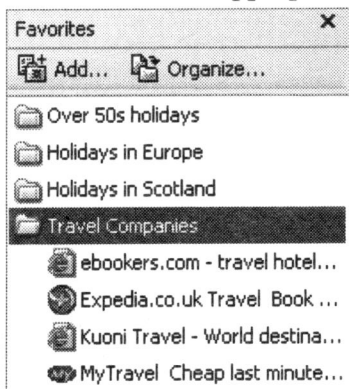

Now, whenever you want to revisit a Web site, simply open up the folder in **Favorites** and click the entry for the site.

Revisiting Web Sites -The History Feature

Links to sites you have visited in recent days are recorded automatically in the **History** feature. As discussed later in this chapter, you can set the number of days for which links are kept. To have a look at your **History** list click the **History** icon on the right of the Internet Explorer Toolbar, shown right and below.

History

The **History** feature opens up in a panel on the left of the screen as shown below. Click each day of the week to see what Web sites have been visited.

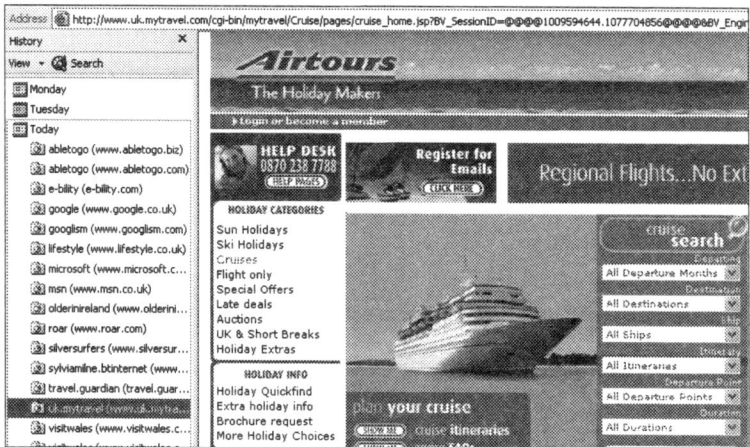

To return to a previously visited Web site, click its link in the **History** panel, as shown on the right. If you are working *offline*, some of the Web pages may be available without connecting to the Internet. Otherwise, if a page is not available, you will be invited to connect to the Internet to view the Web page online.

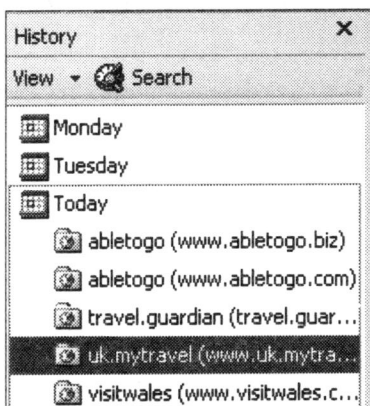

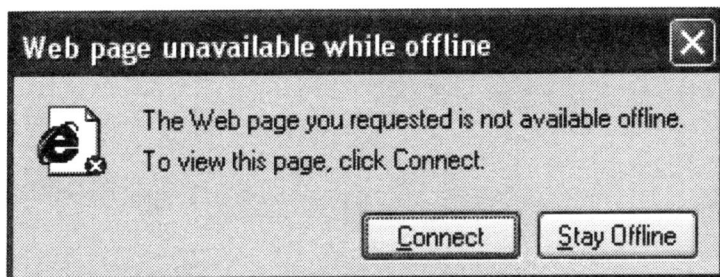

History   ✕

View ▾ 🔍 Search

- 🗓 Monday
- 🗓 Tuesday
- 🗓 Today
  - 🌐 abletogo (www.abletogo.biz)
  - 🌐 abletogo (www.abletogo.com)
  - 🌐 travel.guardian (travel.guar...)
  - 🌐 uk.mytravel (www.uk.mytra...)
  - 🌐 visitwales (www.visitwales.c...)

Web page unavailable while offline   ✕

The Web page you requested is not available offline. To view this page, click Connect.

[Connect]   [Stay Offline]

Keeping and Clearing Links in the History Feature

As mentioned earlier you can set the number of days to keep links in the **History** feature. From the menu bar along the top of Internet Explorer, select **Tools** and **Internet Options....** The **Internet Options** dialogue box opens up with the **General** tab selected, as shown on the next page.

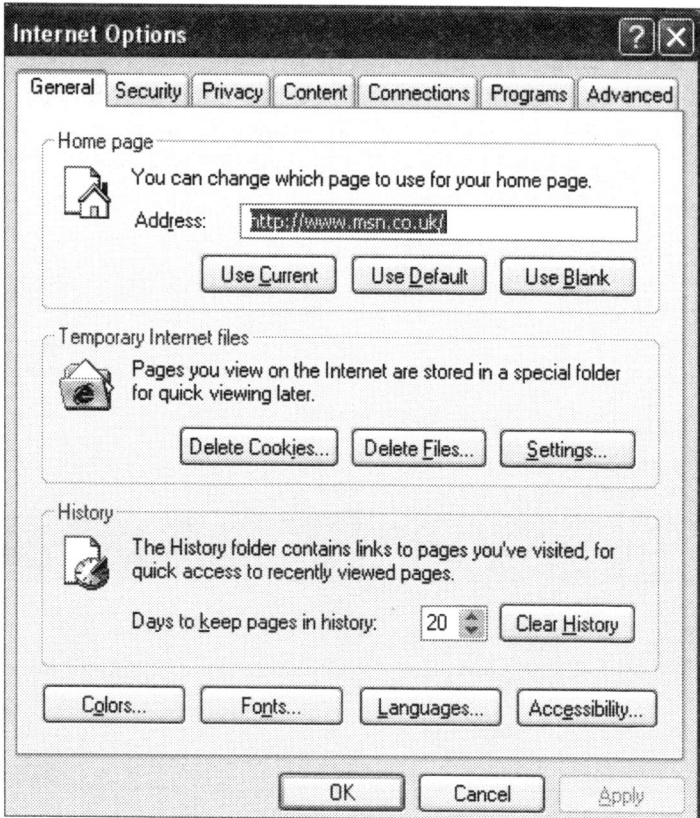

At the bottom of the **Internet Options** dialogue box shown above is a small box for setting the number of days to keep links in the **History** feature. As shown below there is also a **Clear History** button to remove all of the links saved.

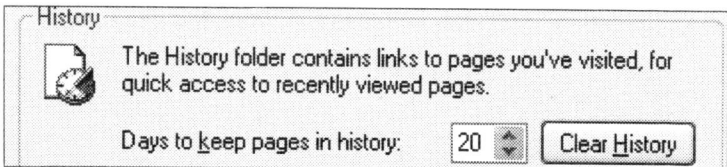

Further Useful Internet Options

It's convenient to digress slightly at this point and mention two useful features which appear on the **Internet Options** window shown on the previous page. These are the option to change your home page and also the option to delete temporary files saved while browsing various Web sites.

Changing Your Home Page

At the top of the **Internet Options** dialogue box shown on the previous page is a box which allows you to change your **Home page**, also shown below. As mentioned earlier, this is the page which your browser normally opens each time you start a session by connecting to the Internet.

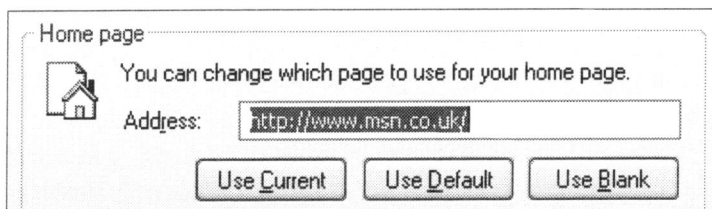

To change your **Home page**, type the address of the new page in the **Address:** bar as shown above, then click **Apply**.

Deleting Temporary Files

While working on the Internet, a lot of *temporary files* are saved on your hard disc. These can be removed to save disc space, using the **Delete Cookies...** and **Delete Files...** buttons shown below, which appear in the middle of the **Internet Options** dialogue box shown on the previous page.

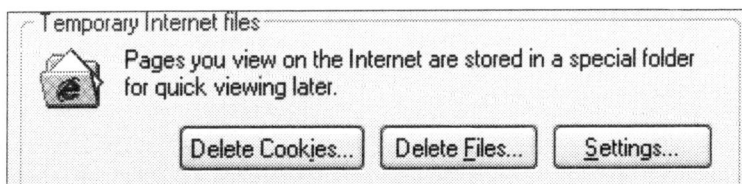

Deleting Cookies

Web sites save certain information, known as *cookies*, on your hard disc. This might include your holiday and travel preferences and pages visited; also personal details such as name, address, e-mail address, etc. The cookies are used to customize the site for you personally, next time you visit.

Deleting Temporary Internet Files

Web sites save certain parts of their Web pages such as graphics, on your hard disc. To save time, next time you visit the Web site, the files are opened from your hard disc. This is faster than downloading from the Internet.

If hard disc space is low, both temporary files and cookies can be deleted, using the **Delete Cookies...** and **Delete Files...** buttons shown on the previous page.

The **Settings** button, shown on the previous page, opens the **Settings** dialogue box, shown below. A slider allows you to adjust the amount of disc space used for **Temporary Internet Files** and there are some *radio buttons*, shown below, to ensure that the latest versions of Web pages are displayed.

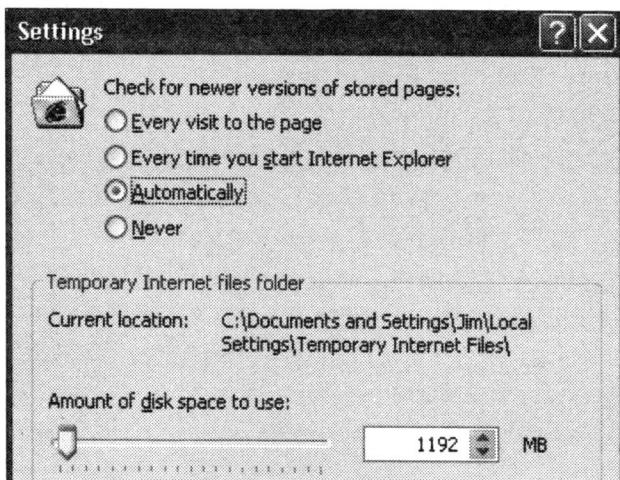

Creating a Shortcut to a Web Site

If you find a Web site that you are likely to return to regularly, you can place a *shortcut icon* on the Windows Desktop (the screen which appears when you first start up the computer). Then, whenever you want to connect to the site, you simply double-click the icon.

For example, suppose you want to return regularly to the Web site of the Hadrian's Wall Tourism Partnership:

www.hadrians-wall.org

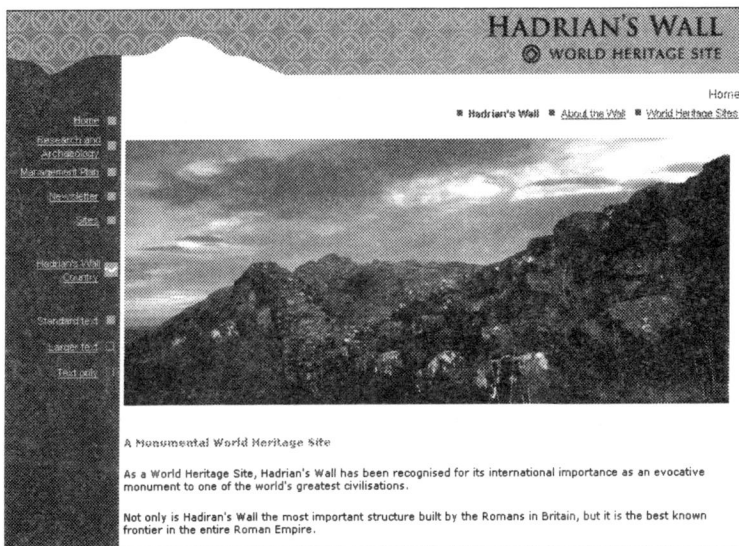

With the Web page displayed on the screen, *right-click* over the page, (but not over a picture). From the menu which appears select the **Create Shortcut** option. This places an icon for the Web site on the Windows Desktop. *Double-click* this icon whenever you want to return directly to the Hadrian's Wall World Heritage Site.

Saving Information from Web Pages

Previous pages in this chapter discussed the way the *links* to Web pages can be saved using **Favorites**, also known as *bookmarks*. These allow you to connect to the Internet and return to a Web site visited previously. In some cases Web pages are saved on the hard disc inside of your computer so that you can view them offline in **Favorites**, as discussed earlier. It's also possible to save information from Web pages manually on your hard disc. The information saved might be a whole Web page consisting of text and graphics; alternatively you can save extracts from a page including pieces of text or individual pictures. This might be useful:

- If you were trying to organize a holiday for a club or local group, say, you could copy and "paste" travel and holiday information from the Internet into a word processing document. This could be used to produce posters or advertisements for the holiday, perhaps in a local newsletter or magazine.

- Travel and holiday information copied from the Internet could be sent to a friend or colleague, as an e-mail *attachment*, during the planning of a joint holiday.

- You can print travel and holiday Web pages on paper, for discussions with other people, away from the computer.

- You might research the area around your holiday destination. Then you could print out maps, notes on places of interest and other useful information to take with you on the trip.

Saving a Web Page on Your Hard Disc

When you are connected to the Internet, with the required page displayed on the screen in Internet Explorer, select **File** and **Save As....** The **Save Web Page** window opens up as shown below. Then enter your own name for the file in the **File name** slot shown below, to replace the default name which Internet Explorer provides automatically.

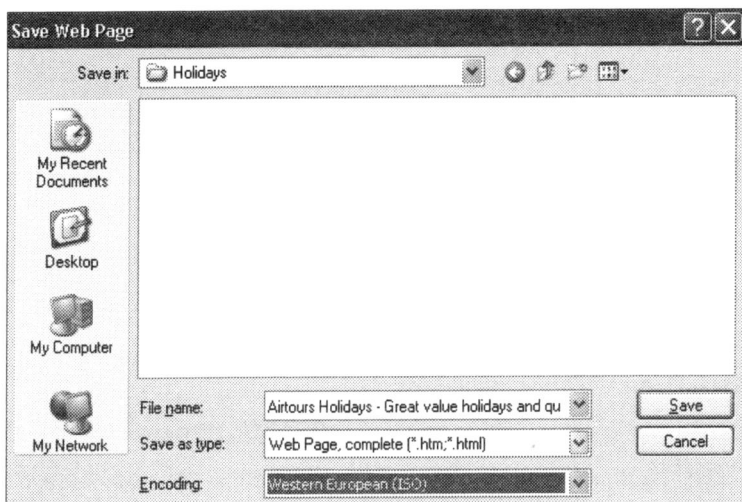

Please note in the above **Save Web Page** window, the file is being saved in a folder called **Holidays**. You can create your own folders such as **Holidays in Britain**, **Holidays in Europe**, **Holidays in Asia**, etc. Click the **Create New Folder** icon as shown right and on the top right of the above **Save Web Page** window. Then type the name of your new folder into the **New Folder** slot, as shown below.

Web pages can be saved in any one of several formats using the **Save as type:** drop-down menu as shown in the extract from the **Save Web Page** dialogue box below.

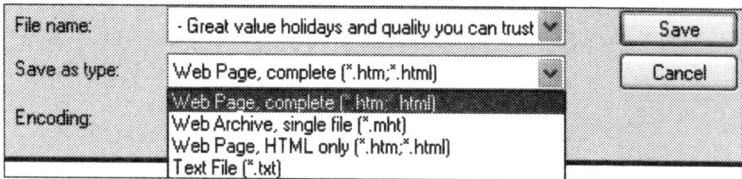

File name:	- Great value holidays and quality you can trust ✔	Save
Save as type:	Web Page, complete (*.htm;*.html) ✔	Cancel
Encoding:	Web Page, complete (*.htm;.html)	
	Web Archive, single file (*.mht)	
	Web Page, HTML only (*.htm;*.html)	
	Text File (*.txt)	

These file types include:

Web Page, complete (*.htm, *.html)

This format saves everything on the page, i.e. text, graphics files and any sound files, etc.

Web Archive, single file (*.mht)

This takes a snapshot of the Web page and saves it as a single file.

Web Page, HTML only (*.htm, *.html)

This option saves only the text, in HTML format.

Web pages saved in the above formats can be viewed offline at a later date, in a Web browser such as Internet Explorer. (The browser can be set to work offline using the main **File** menu.)

Text File (*.txt)

This is plain text without any of the formatting features built into pages in the HTML language. A **Text File** is universally acceptable to other programs such as word processors and simple text editors like Notepad and WordPad, included with the Microsoft Windows operating system.

In the following example I have saved a complete Web page with the name **Destinations**. This is shown below in the Windows Explorer. To start the Windows Explorer, *right-click* over the *start* button then left-click **Explore** from the menu which pops up.

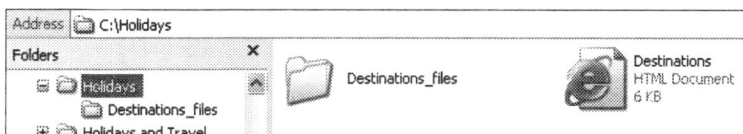

The entry for the Web page is shown above right as an **HTML Document** with the name **Destinations**. You can also see that the file is stored in the **Holidays** folder on the **C:** drive. (**C:** is the usual label for the hard disc inside your computer). If you now double-click the **Destinations** icon shown above in the Windows Explorer, Internet Explorer opens up with the **Destinations** Web page displayed on the screen, as shown below.

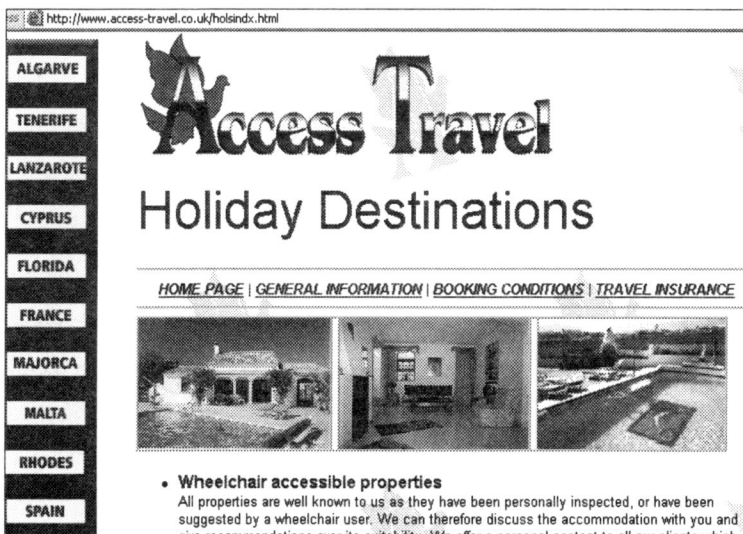

Saving a Picture from a Web Page

While connected online to the Internet, with your browser displaying the required Web page, *right-click* over the picture to be saved. A menu appears including the option to save the picture in a folder of your choice.

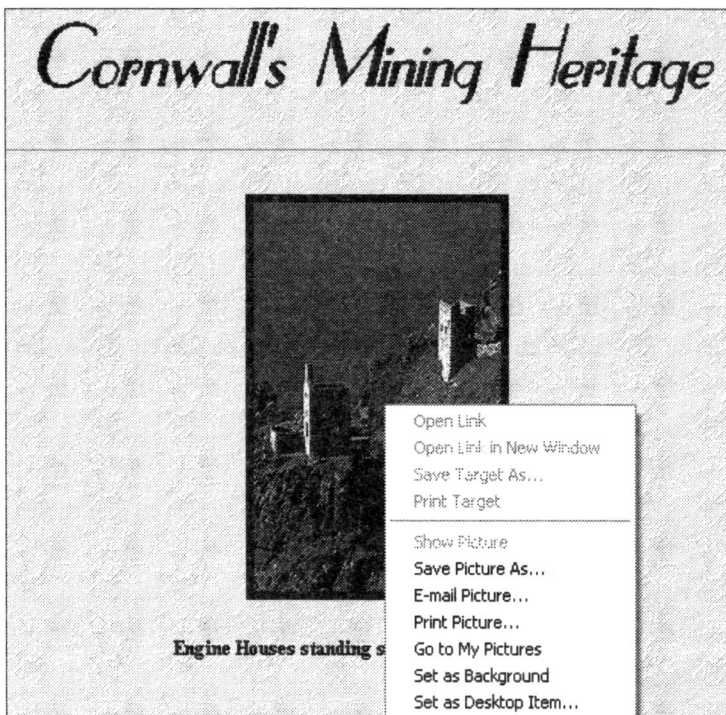

There are also options, as shown on the menu above, to create a shortcut from the Windows Desktop to the Web page or to use the picture as a background on your Windows Desktop.

Select **Save Picture As...** from the menu which appears, as shown on the previous page. This leads to the **Save Picture** dialogue box shown below. Here you can enter a name for the picture and save it in a picture file type such as **JPEG** (**.jpg**), shown below. **JPEG** is very suitable if you want to send a picture as an *attachment* to an e-mail.

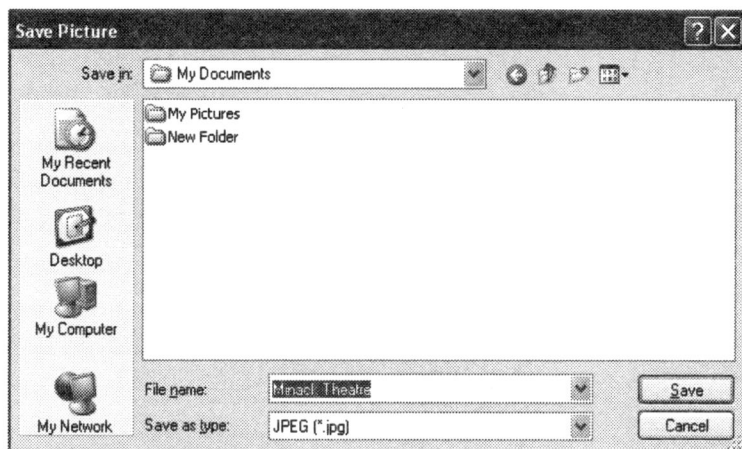

After saving, the picture can be opened for viewing offline. **JPEG** picture files can be opened in **Paint**, a program which is supplied as a free accessory to Microsoft Windows. To launch **Paint** select *Start*, **All Programs**, **Accessories** and **Paint**, as shown below.

Shown below is a picture from the Cornish mining industry, captured from the Internet and displayed in **Paint**.

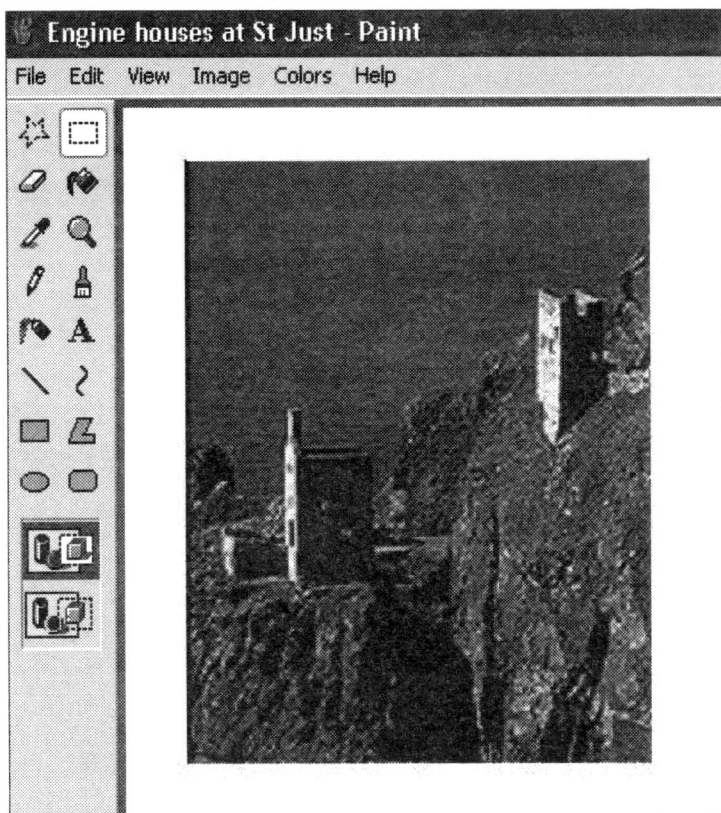

A copy of the picture can easily be printed using **File** and **Print...** from a program like **Paint**. You might also include the picture in a word processing document or send it as an attachment to an e-mail.

Obviously anyone intending to reproduce Web material commercially should first obtain permission from the owners of the Web site.

Saving Part of a Web Page - Cut and Paste

To copy a piece of text from a Web page, a simple method is as follows:

- Select, i.e. highlight with the mouse, the required text on the Web page.

- Click **Edit** and select **Copy** from the menu. This puts a copy of the piece of text onto the Windows *clipboard*, a temporary store for holding text and graphics.

- Open the destination for the Web page extract. This might be a Microsoft Word document, for example.

- Select **Edit** and **Paste** to place the Web page extract onto the page in the document, which can now be saved and printed, etc.

Another useful method is to press the **Print Screen** key while displaying the required Web page. This places a copy of the entire screen onto the clipboard, from where it can be pasted into a program like Word or Paint.

contours WALKING HOLIDAYS
Walking Holidays in Scotland, England, Wales and Ireland

Home | Walking Holidays in Britain and Ireland | About our walking holidays | Group Discounts and Tailor-made Tours | Contact Us | Booking | Links | Testimonials

Welcome

Contours Walking Holidays are *the* specialists in self-guided walking holidays (hiking tours) in Scotland, England, Wales and Ireland. Within this web site you'll find an unrivalled range of walking holidays along more than fifty trails in Britain ranging from famous routes like Hadrian's Wall Path, West Highland Way, Wainwright's Coast to Coast Walk, Cotswold Way, Offa's Dyke Path, Cumbria Way, Pembrokeshire Coast Path or the Dales Way to little-known gems like Northumberland's Coast of Castles, Edge of Wales Walk, Wild Edric's Way, Cotswold Villages Trail or the Three Castles Walk.

Whatever your interest - following in the footsteps of Roman Legionnaires along Hadrians Wall, hiking from coast to coast across England, tracing the route of cattle drovers through the Highlands of Scotland, walking the coastline of Cornwall, following a river on its journey from source to sea, climbing England's highest mountain in the Lake District, studying seabirds from the cliffs of the Pembrokeshire Coast Path or exploring villages in the Cotswolds - our extensive range of walking tours means you'll be sure to find your

Hadrian's Wall

Coast to Coast Walk

Printing a Web Page

Internet Explorer has an option to print Web pages. From the menu select **File** and **Print**.... It's a good idea to use the **File** and **Print Preview...** option to see in advance how a Web page will print out on paper. The **Print** dialogue box appears over the Web page as shown on the right below.

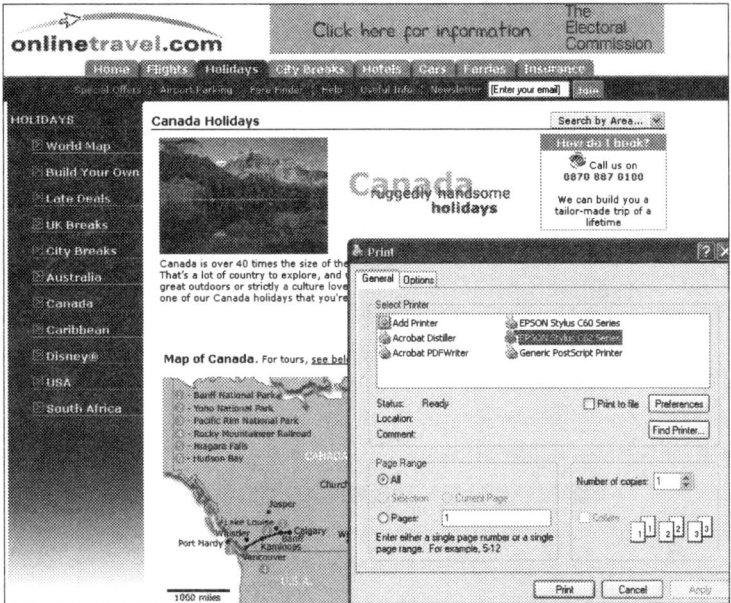

If you have problems printing while online, try some of the methods described on the previous pages. For example, select all or part of a page then use **Edit** and **Copy** in the browser to place the information on the clipboard, before using **Edit** and **Paste** to put the Web information into a word processor like Microsoft Word. Then you can print the information like any other word processing document.

5

Arranging Travel by Road and Sea

Among the advantages of making travel arrangements online, using the Internet, are the following:

- You can study time-tables, etc., in your own home, instead of visiting bus stations, etc., or trying to write down information while on the telephone.

- The information on a Web site should be completely up to date, with the latest prices.

- You can obtain information from lots of different competing travel companies, compare prices and obtain last-minute deals and special offers.

- Some travel companies give discounts and promotions exclusive to customers booking online.

- The Internet is *interactive*, allowing tickets to be booked online and information to be printed out.

- You can find and print the best route for a road journey, including places en route, road junctions, distances and maps. Alternative routes via certain places or suitable for caravans can be printed.

This chapter describes the use of the Internet for arranging journeys by road and sea; rail travel and flights are discussed in detail in the next two chapters.

Travelling by Coach

There are many advantages to travelling by coach, particularly for older people. It's one of the easiest types of holiday, since everything is done for you. Some coach operators arrange for you to be picked up from home and your bags are carried at every stage of the journey to your hotel room. Unlike a journey by plane, you are spared the inconvenience of carrying your luggage around a busy airport and checking in and waiting for flights, which may be delayed.

A well-organised coach journey will include regular stops for refreshment and exercise. The coach driver often doubles up as a knowledgeable tour guide, knowing the best places to visit from past experience. You are relieved of the headaches of route finding, car parking and aggressive motorway drivers. If you are going into Europe, you will also be spared the need to arrange ferry crossings and the driver will probably allow you to take advantage of the best duty-free shops.

National Express Coaches

National Express is one of the main coach operators running scheduled services between major cities in the UK and Ireland. In partnership with other European coaching companies, National Express also offers short breaks in destinations in Europe, such as Paris and Amsterdam.

National Express gives generous discounts for older passengers, who make up a large proportion of coach travellers. For example, if you're over 50 you can obtain a National Express **Advantage50 Discount Coachcard**, giving 30% off the fare on many journeys.

Cost £10 for 1 year or £19 for 3 years.

If you are over the age of 50, you can enjoy the benefits of an Advantage50 Discount Coachcard, giving you savings of up to 30% on many National Express coaches. Throughout the year, holders of discount coachcards will also receive a variety of exclusive offers.

Advantage50 Discount Coachcards cost just £10 for one year & £19 for a three year card, click here to buy online now ⊛

If you're over 60, the **routesixty** scheme from National Express offers savings of up to 50% on most journeys.

routesixty

National Express

Home | What is routesixty? | How to book | Your questions answered | Register

over sixty? 1/2 price fares

What is routesixty?

If you are 60 or above, then you are entitled to travel for up to half price on all National Express routes almost all of the time. All we ask is that you book your ticket at least one day before you travel.

National Express half price fares are available on normal adult fare journeys at any day of the week except Fridays. In July and August, Fridays and Saturdays are exempt from the half price offer. On those days, you automatically qualify for a discounted fare of up to 30% off. The level of discount is dependent on the route used.

If you buy a ticket on the day of travel you qualify for a discounted fare of up to 30%.

Please note: National Express half price fares do not apply to APEX or any other promotional fares.

To get the full discount, please remember...

• You must be 60 or over

www.nationalexpress.com

Wallace Arnold Coaches

Wallace Arnold is one of the best known holiday operators, operating luxury coaches across the United Kingdom, Ireland and Europe. Wallace Arnold picks up passengers from points from all over Britain. Their Grand Tourer coaches offer almost 50% more leg room and include an on-board lounge with reading facilities and stereo music. Wallace Arnold offers a large choice of holidays and hotels in a wide variety of locations.

To book your Wallace Arnold holiday online you simply select the area of Britain in which you live, choose a destination and a holiday then click **Book Here** to open up the online booking form. After entering your name and details of your party, dates, etc., click the **Submit** button to complete the booking and choose a departure point.

www.wallacearnold.com

Shearings Coaches

This company is one of the largest UK coach and holiday companies and has its own hotels all over Britain. Holidays can be booked online and are also arranged worldwide, to destinations such as Australia, New Zealand, China, Canada and the USA. Shearings also offers a wide range of special interest holidays, a small sample of which is shown below. These include many activities which may be of interest to some older people, such as antiques, bridge, classical music, ballroom and sequence dancing.

www.shearingsholidays.com

antiques

Explore the world of wonderful, fine crafted antiques in the company of experts and fellow enthusiasts.
Click here to book online

bridge

With experts on hand to help you develop your game at any level from beginner to old hand. Equipment provided.
Click here to book online

music appreciation

Explore the backgrounds and lives of your favourite composers whilst staying in the area that inspired their work.
Click here to book online

dancing

A choice of sequence or salsa based dancing breaks at carefully selected hotels with breathtakingly elegant ballrooms.
Click here to book online

self-guided walking

Designed for the independent traveller to explore the beautiful scenery of the British countryside.
Click here to book online

guided walking

Explore the beautiful scenery of the British countryside on a guided walking holiday led by an expert .
Click here to book online

Coach Travel for Seniors

A lot of coach travel sites of interest to older people can be found by entering suitable keywords into Google, such as:

At the top of the list of search results is a link to the Yahoo! Directory **Seniors**, shown below.

The above directory contains links to organizations providing travel and holidays for older people. These Web sites offer a full range of holidays and travel, not just coach travel.

Clicking one of the links, **Travel 55** for example, opens up a Web site offering all sorts of holidays to European and worldwide destinations.

www.travel55.co.uk

The **Travel 55** site includes a link, **Coach Holidays**, which emphasizes the relaxing nature of this type of holiday, as shown below. This Web site includes a comprehensive list of coach companies offering holidays particularly suitable for the over 50s. A small extract from the list of coach companies is shown below.

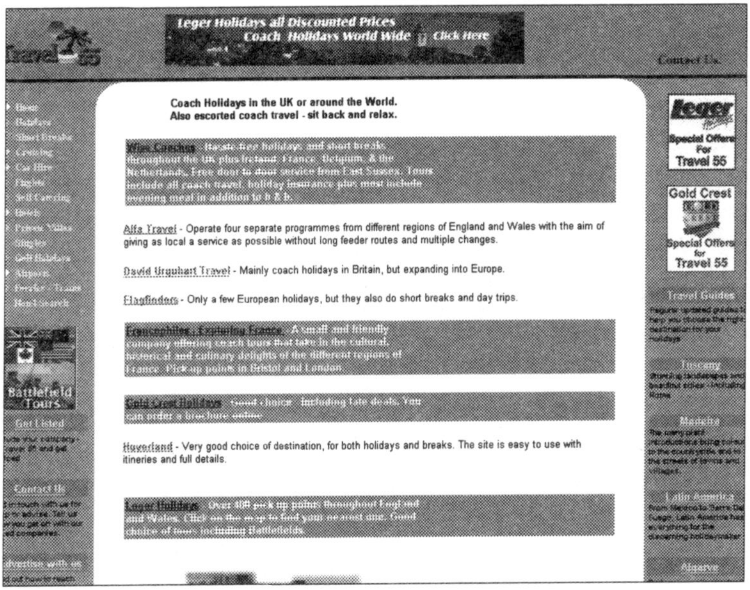

Click on any of the links, shown underlined above, to open up the Web sites of the various coach companies. These give details of coaching holidays in Britain and Europe with information such as the destinations, hotels, prices and local pick-up points.

Coach Travel and Holidays for the Disabled

A number of companies specialize in organizing coach travel and holidays for the disabled and elderly. Entering some keywords such as **coach travel disabled** into Google, as previously described, brings up a list of relevant Web sites. For example, John Flanagan Coach Travel of Warrington provides coach trips and holidays for the disabled, using "wheelchair friendly" coaches.

www.flanagancoaches.co.uk

Eurobility.com Travel is a Web site providing links to a complete range of holidays, coach companies and hotels providing facilities for the disabled or elderly traveller. The site includes a link to **DisChat**, an online forum which allows you to air your thoughts about disability issues.

www.eurobility.com/travel

The **DisChat** forum also includes a link to **UK Coach Travel**, a **Web** site which gives online booking facilities for journeys with 2,500 companies having 15,000 coaches.

www.ukcoachtravel.com

Planning Your Own Road Journey

If you are travelling by car, etc., around Britain, Ireland and Europe you can obtain help with planning your route, using one of a number of programs available free on the Internet. These can be found by entering, for example, the keywords **route finder** into Google, as discussed earlier in this book.

One of these programs is **AA Route Planner**, for example. First you enter the place you are starting **From** and then the place you are going **To**, as shown below. Obviously if there are other places with the same name, then additional information such as the county will be useful. The places can also be specified as a post code, street name, motorway or road junction or a place of interest, such as the **Eden Project**, for example. The **Via** box shown below allows you to specify a particular place to be included in the route.

© Automobile Association Developments Limited 2004
Boxes at the bottom of the screen allow you to find routes for caravans or avoiding motorways and toll roads, etc.

5   Arranging Travel by Road and Sea

When you click the **Next** button shown above, the program asks you to confirm the entries in the **From** and **To** slots. If you are not sure that a place is the one you want, click the **Check on a Map** button for further information. When you are happy with the place of departure and the destination, click **Next** and the program works out the best route.

Just**AA**sk.   [   ] [Search >]
Home | AA Services | Motoring | Travel & Leisure | Car Buyer's Guide | Contact Us
Route Planner | European Breakdown Cover | Travel Bookshop | Travel Insurance | Hotels & B&Bs

Home

Motoring
Travel & Leisure
Services

Contact us

A to Z

Route Planner
Here are the results of your route

Summary and turn-by-turn directions for your route

From: Land's End,Cnwll
To: John O'Groats,Highld

Total Distance: 852.5 miles (convert to kilometres)
Total Time: 16 hr 48 min

LONDON

Street by Street Atlases
Save 20% online

View a map of your route | Reverse this route | New route | Printer friendly page

Going on a long trip?   The cost of your journey   Email newsletter
Remember to service your   Use our driving cost   Be the first to hear about
car before you set off.   calculator to work it out.   special offers. Sign-up here

Acc.	Dist	Route	Directions
0.00	0.00	**A30**	Start out at Land's End,Cnwll Follow the Penzance road A30
1.00	1.00	**A30**	Sennen (church)
4.00	3.00	**A30**	Crows-an-wra

© Automobile Association Developments Limited 2004

As shown above, the program calculates the total distance in miles (or kilometres if required) and the total time. The route is listed with place names, road junctions and islands and distances. You can even calculate an approximate cost of the journey and display a map of the route. The listing of the places on the route and the map can be printed on paper, to take with you on the journey.

www.theaa.com/travelwatch/planner_main.jsp

Help for Disabled Drivers

A number of Web sites support disabled drivers, including the sites of the Disabled Drivers' Motor Club and the Disabled Drivers' Association.

The Disabled Drivers Motor Club

This site gives news about activities such as the Baywatch campaign to secure better help with parking. The club also obtains discounts on ferry travel, insurance and car spares for the disabled motorist. Links are provided to numerous Web sites giving help with disability and mobility matters. These include **youreable.com**, which gives advice on issues such as the Motability Scheme helping the disabled motorist to lease or buy a car. There is also a Caravan and Campers Section.

www.ddmc.org.uk

The Disabled Drivers Association

This organization has a Web site campaigning for disabled drivers, promoting causes such as the Blue Badge scheme giving parking concessions. There are links to news pages, other sites helping disabled people, discounts on products and help with the sale of specially modified vehicles. The Disabled Drivers Association has long-standing arrangements for full members to receive substantial discounts from the car ferry companies for travel to and from the continent and within the British Isles.

www.dda.org.uk

Cruises

The CenNet site is a good place to start and includes every type of cruise, ranging from the Caledonian Discovery, cruising in the Scottish Highlands, to barge and narrowboat holidays in Britain and Europe, to luxury cruises all over the world, with companies such as P&O.

www.cennet.co.uk

The Saga Group provides a wide range of services for the over 50s, with a complete range of holidays including cruises on oceans, rivers and fjords, aboard their own ships **Saga Rose** and **Saga Pearl**. Various Saga cruises circumnavigate the world and places visited include Australia, South Africa, Brazil and France as well as Iceland and Antarctica.

www.saga.co.uk

Shown below is P&O Cruises' superliner Aurora capable of carrying nearly 2000 passengers on world-wide cruises from the UK

AURORA: Britain's new superliner for the new Millennium

P&O Cruises

P&O Cruises' 76,000-ton ship Aurora arrived in spring of 2000.

Britain's new superliner for the new millennium cost £200 million and was built, like the highly successful Oriana, at the Meyer Werft Shipyard in Germany.

The ship carries more than 1,850 passengers on a wide range of world-wide cruise itineraries from the UK. She is a sister ship to Oriana, introduced as the P&O flagship in April 1995, and boasts significant advances in design, including

- Five decks of cabins with private balconies
- A business centre
- A retractable magradome over the midships swimming pool

Cruise.com

This American site states that it's the world's largest database of cruises. The site has comprehensive search facilities for cruises all over the world and there are special deals and links to compare prices with other travel companies. The Web site includes interviews with a large number of the **cruise.com** staff about their experiences organizing and participating in a variety of cruises.

www.cruise.com

There are links to cruises for various special purposes such as luxury cruises, cruises for singles and those with special needs. Some cruise ships have especially accessible rooms and facilities suitable for the disabled and may also allow passengers to be accompanied by guide dogs.

Ferry Services

If you are travelling to Europe, Ireland, The Isles of Man or Skye, etc., then a ferry is the main alternative to flying, particularly if you are taking a vehicle with you. The Internet provides lots of Web sites enabling ferries to be booked online. **ferrybooker.com** allows you to search through a list of companies to find a ferry matching your particular requirements of place of departure, destination, travelling times and the number of people in your party.

When a suitable ferry is found you are given a quotation before proceeding to the online booking system to enter your personal details and pay for the trip, using your credit card. If you are taking a vehicle, your booking details must include the vehicle's approximate height and length.

www.ferrybooker.com

Please also see the related site:

www.onlinetravel.com

The Seaview Web site has links to the major cruise and ferry services around the British Isles and Europe, with online booking.

This site contains a number of interesting links including Webcams on ships around the world, as shown below. Pictures are updated at regular intervals, together with details of the ship's position, speed and the weather.

www.seaview.co.uk

The Channel Tunnel

Eurotunnel allows cars, caravans, coaches, and passengers, etc., to cross the Channel between Folkestone and Calais in a mere 35 minutes.

You can check the availability of departures to match your required travel dates and times, obtain a quotation and make a booking online using your credit card. There are also links to information about short breaks in France, travel insurance and French food.

www.eurotunnel.com

Arranging Rail Travel

The National Rail Web Site

The main source of Internet rail travel information in Britain is the National Rail Web site, whose home page, shown below, has the following address:

www.nationalrail.co.uk

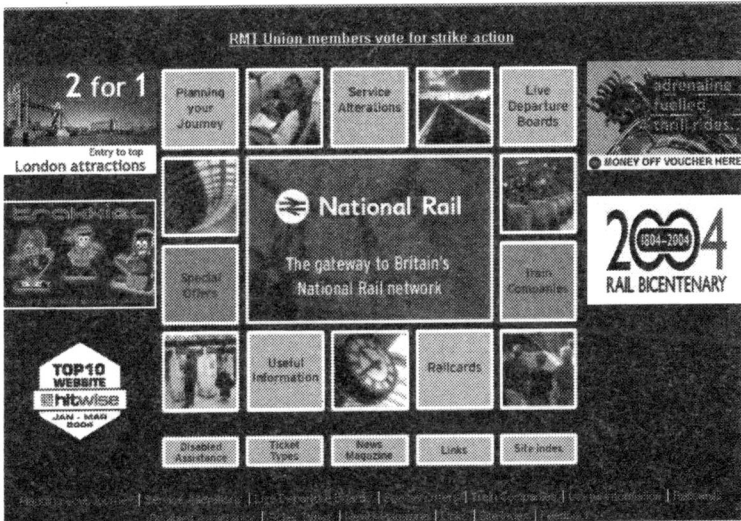

The National Rail Web site is provided by ATOC, The Association of Train Operating Companies.

Navigating the National Rail Web Site

The Web site is navigated by clicking on any of the square links arranged around the National Rail logo in the centre of the screen. For example, if you click **Useful Information**, as shown on the previous page, the following page appears.

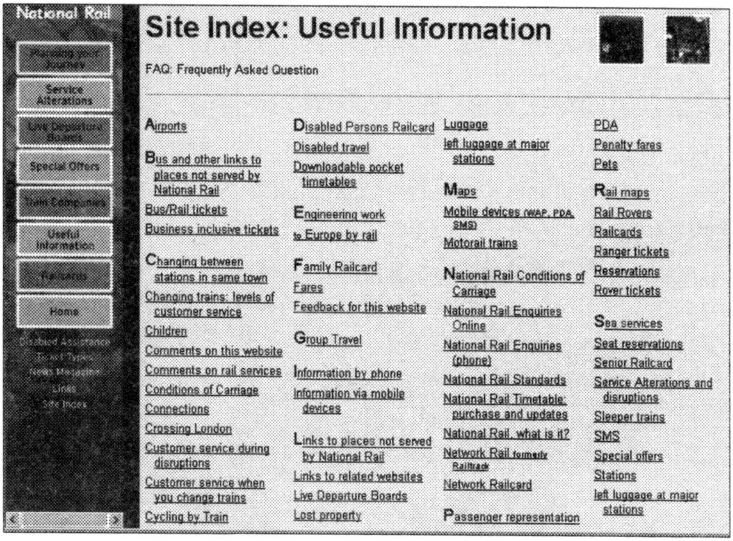

The **Site Index** shown above is a comprehensive list of links to further Web pages of useful information, which should provide answers to most travellers questions. A small extract from the **Site Index** is shown enlarged below.

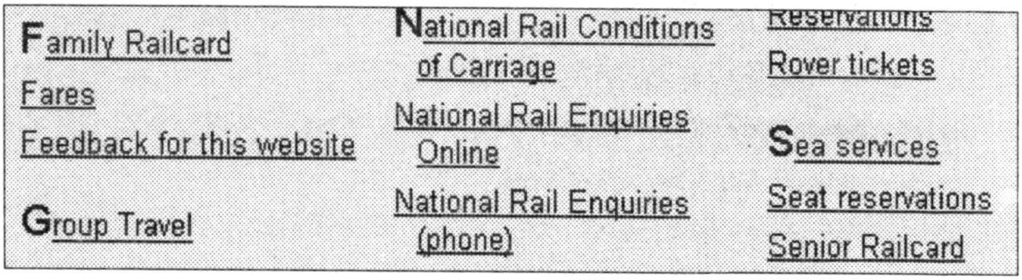

When you leave the National Rail home page shown on page 89 and select a new page such as the **Useful Information** page, the links to the other main pages are displayed down the left-hand side of the screen. **Planning your Journey** allows you to enter your travelling times and destination and obtain tickets. This feature is discussed in more detail shortly.

Service Alterations displays a list of routes affected by engineering work, etc., and gives times and alternative arrangements.

The **Live Departure Boards** link allows you to locate a particular station and to see an up-to-date list of departures. You can enter part of the station name or select from a drop-down list based on the first letter. Every station has a 3-letter code. Entering this will find the station more quickly. (3-letter codes are displayed against the list of station names which appears, as shown below).

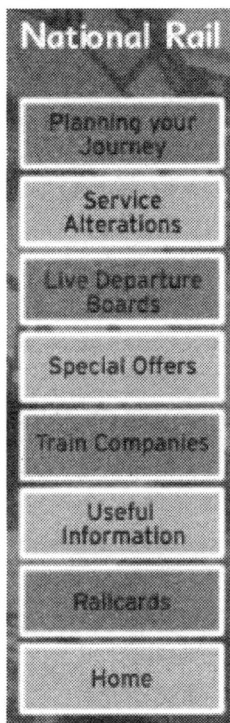

Search for your station

Find my station

A B C D E F G H I J K L M N O P Q R S T U V W X Y Z

You searched for MA. Here is a list of matching stations followed by their 3 letter codes

MACCLESFIELD (MAC)	MACHYNLLETH (MCN)	MAESTEG (EWENNY ROAD) (MEW)
MAESTEG STATION (MST)	MAGHULL (MAG)	MAIDEN NEWTON (MDN)

Special Offers

The **Special Offers** link on the previous page presents a list of train operating companies. Clicking on one of these companies lists their current special offers and promotions.

For example, at the time of writing, the Midland Mainline promotions included a trip from London to Chatsworth House in the Peak District.

Booking arrangements for these special offers can be found on the train operating company's Web site, using the **Train Companies** link discussed below.

Train Operating Companies

The **Train Companies** link, shown on the right, presents a list of all of the main **Train Operating Companies (TOCs)** in Britain. When you click on the name of a company you are presented with a page displaying details of the company. These include the key personnel, postal address, Web address and telephone numbers, etc., as shown below for the First Great Western Web site.

National Rail Enquiries

First Great Western

First **Great Western**
transforming travel

First Great Western

Company information	
Managing Director / CEO	Alison Forster
Phone number	01793 499400
Fax number	01793 49 94 00
Postal address	Head Office Milford House 1 Milford Street Swindon SN1 1HL
Website	http://www.firstgreatwestern.co.uk/
Support & information	

Railcards

The **Railcards** link shown on the right connects to a separate Web site, **www.railcard.co.uk**, where you can buy a variety of discount cards, depending on your circumstances.

The Senior Railcard

If you're aged 60 or over, the Senior Railcard gives substantial discounts off most First Class and Standard fares in England, Scotland and Wales. The card costs £20 and is valid for one year.

www.railcard.co.uk   **www.senior-railcard.co.uk**

The Disabled Persons Railcard

Anyone who qualifies for the Disabled Persons Railcard can buy rail tickets at up to one third off the full price. At the time of writing, the Disabled Persons Railcard costs £14 and is valid for one year. Anyone travelling with a disabled person also qualifies for the discounted fare.

www.disabledpersons-railcard.co.uk

Eligibility

The Disabled Persons Railcard allows you to buy discounted rail tickets. If another adult is travelling with you, they can also travel at the same discounted fare. The Railcard currently costs £14 and is valid for 12 months.

To qualify, you must meet at least one of the criteria listed below. The application form lists the proof you will need to provide to confirm that you are eligible for a Railcard.

You qualify if you:

- are registered as visually impaired;
- are registered deaf;
- have epilepsy, and are disabled by repeated attacks even though you receive drug treatment;
- receive Attendance Allowance;
- receive Disability Living Allowance (in the Higher Rate for help with getting around, or in the Higher or Middle Rate for help with personal care;

Along the bottom of the National Rail home page shown on page 89 are 5 further links, as shown below.

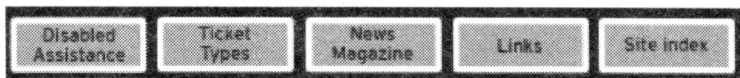

Disabled Assistance leads to a page showing how the train operating companies provide extra help for disabled or mobility-impaired passengers. This can include train operating company staff helping you at the various stations on your journey.

The link **Find your starting station** allows you to enter the name (or part of the name) of a station and check out the facilities. These include car parking, local taxi and bus services, the location of toilets on the station, assistance available for customers and the amount of step-free and level access for disabled people. There is also a link enabling you to download a booklet, **Rail Travel for Disabled Passengers.**

Ticket Types on the menu shown above is a link to Web pages describing the various types of ticket. You are helped to find the best type of ticket to suit your needs and how to buy them - including online purchase over the Internet.

The **News Magazine** link shown above opens up the **Online Traveller** magazine, giving the latest news from the Train Operating Companies.

Clicking **Links** on the menu shown at the top of the page presents a very comprehensive list of links to the Web sites of the Train Operating Companies and related organizations as well as overseas railways.

Planning Your Journey

This is one of the main features of the National Rail Web site. It allows you to check the timetables for trains going to a particular destination from your local station, and gives full details of the times, the itinerary and the prices. After selecting a particular train your details can be passed to another site to purchase the ticket online.

To start planning a journey, click the **Planning your Journey** icon shown on the right. This icon appears on the National Rail home page shown on page 89. Alternatively click the **Planning your Journey** icon on the vertical menu shown on page 91. The **National Rail Enquiries** screen opens as shown below.

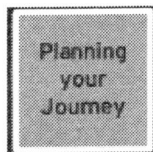

As shown above, the **Leaving from** and **Going to** stations are entered, together with dates and times, for both outward and return journeys, if necessary. You can also specify a limit to the number of changes on the journey.

Now click the arrow next to **Get train times** shown on the previous page. After a short time you are presented with the **Timetable result**, as shown below.

GO BACK

National Rail Enquiries

NEW JOURNEY

Timetable result: Willington to Penzance

Here are the trains that best match your requested journey. Some places may have more than one station. View details to check the actual departure and arrival stations.

*LINKS MARKED AS TUBE, MAY NOT OPERATE LATE AT NIGHT OR EARLY IN THE MORNING PLEASE CHECK WITH THE APPROPRIATE OPERATOR

Outward journey

Friday 28 May 2004

Depart	09:23	10:46
Arrive	16:53	18:01
Changes	2	2
Duration	7:30	7:15

EARLIER TRAIN VIEW DETAILS LATER TRAIN

Return journey

Wednesday 9 June 2004

Depart	09:28	10:08	11:20
Arrive	17:22	17:22	18:17
Changes	1	2	2
Duration	7:54	7:14	6:57

EARLIER TRAIN VIEW DETAILS LATER TRAIN

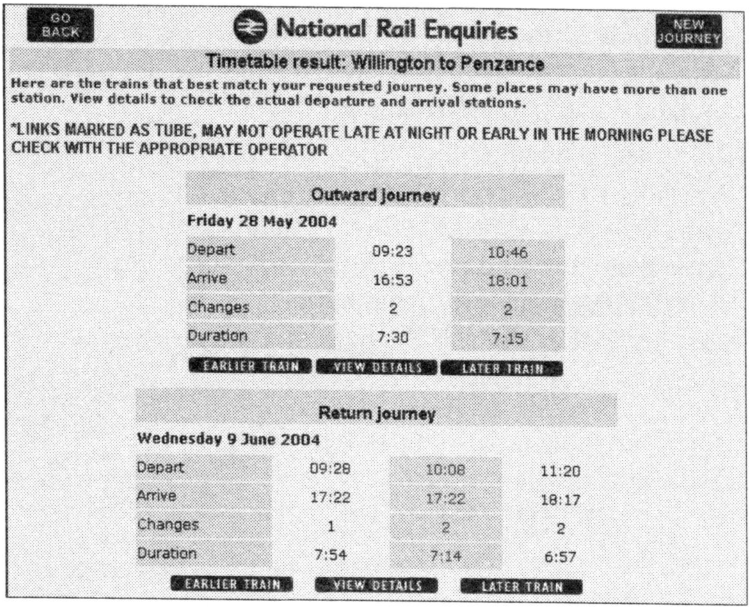

The times for suitable trains for both outward and return journeys are presented and there are buttons to allow you to check earlier and later trains. The **VIEW DETAILS** button displays a list of all of the stations on the route, with times and train operating companies. Details for all of the available trains are shown, including outward and return journeys, as shown in the following extract.

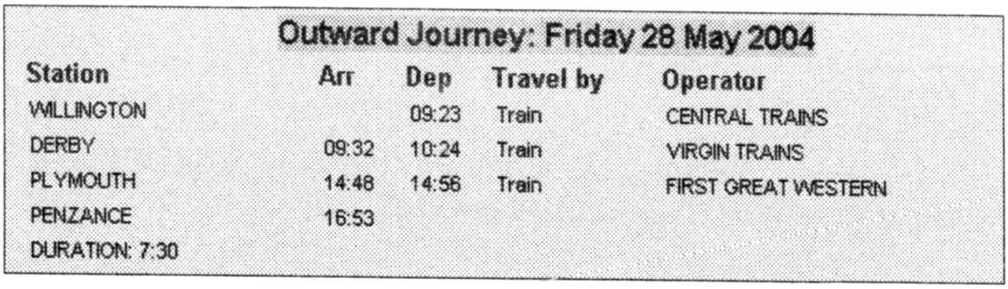

Outward Journey: Friday 28 May 2004

Station	Arr	Dep	Travel by	Operator
WILLINGTON		09:23	Train	CENTRAL TRAINS
DERBY	09:32	10:24	Train	VIRGIN TRAINS
PLYMOUTH	14:48	14:56	Train	FIRST GREAT WESTERN
PENZANCE	16:53			
DURATION: 7:30				

At the bottom of the **Timetable result** screen shown on the previous page is a section for entering passenger details, including any railcards and the type of tickets required.

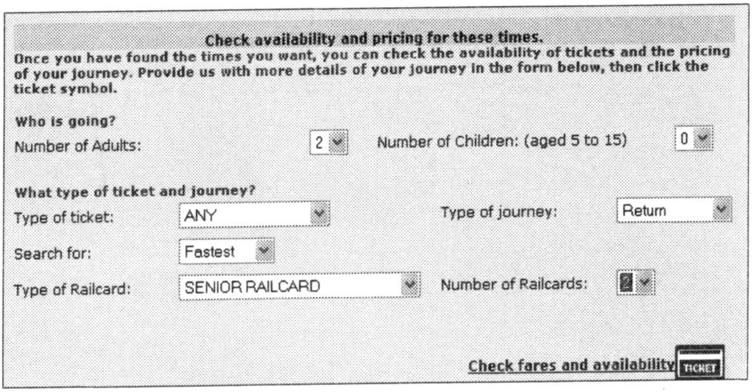

Check availability and pricing for these times.
Once you have found the times you want, you can check the availability of tickets and the pricing of your journey. Provide us with more details of your journey in the form below, then click the ticket symbol.

Who is going?

Number of Adults: `2` Number of Children: (aged 5 to 15) `0`

What type of ticket and journey?

Type of ticket: `ANY` Type of journey: `Return`

Search for: `Fastest`

Type of Railcard: `SENIOR RAILCARD` Number of Railcards: `2`

Check fares and availability `TICKET`

If you now click **Check fares and availability**, a screen appears giving the times of the available trains. Also shown are the prices for different types of ticket, e.g. **SINGLE FARES**, **SAVER RETURN**, etc., as shown on the left below.

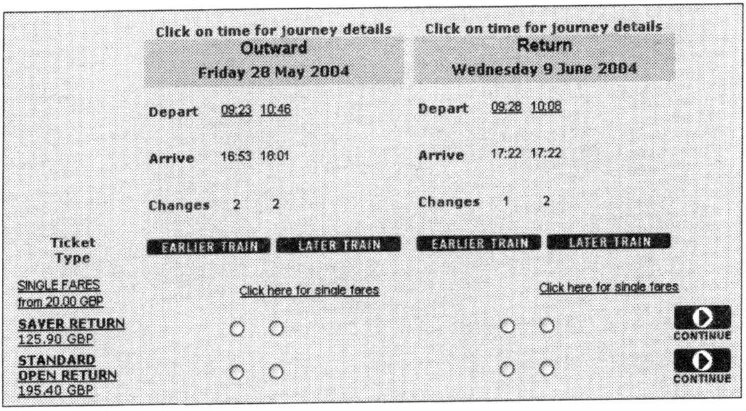

Click on time for journey details
Outward
Friday 28 May 2004

Click on time for journey details
Return
Wednesday 9 June 2004

Depart 09:23 10:46

Depart 09:28 10:08

Arrive 16:53 18:01

Arrive 17:22 17:22

Changes 2 2

Changes 1 2

Ticket Type | EARLIER TRAIN | LATER TRAIN | EARLIER TRAIN | LATER TRAIN

SINGLE FARES from 20.00 GBP — Click here for single fares — Click here for single fares

SAVER RETURN 125.90 GBP — ○ ○ — ○ ○ — CONTINUE

STANDARD OPEN RETURN 195.40 GBP — ○ ○ — ○ ○ — CONTINUE

Now select the ticket type and the train for the outward and return journeys by clicking in two of the above circles.

In the case of single fares, click the link **Click here for single fares** shown on the screenshot on page 97.

Now click the **CONTINUE** button shown on the previous page to display full details of the journey, with stations, times, operators and prices.

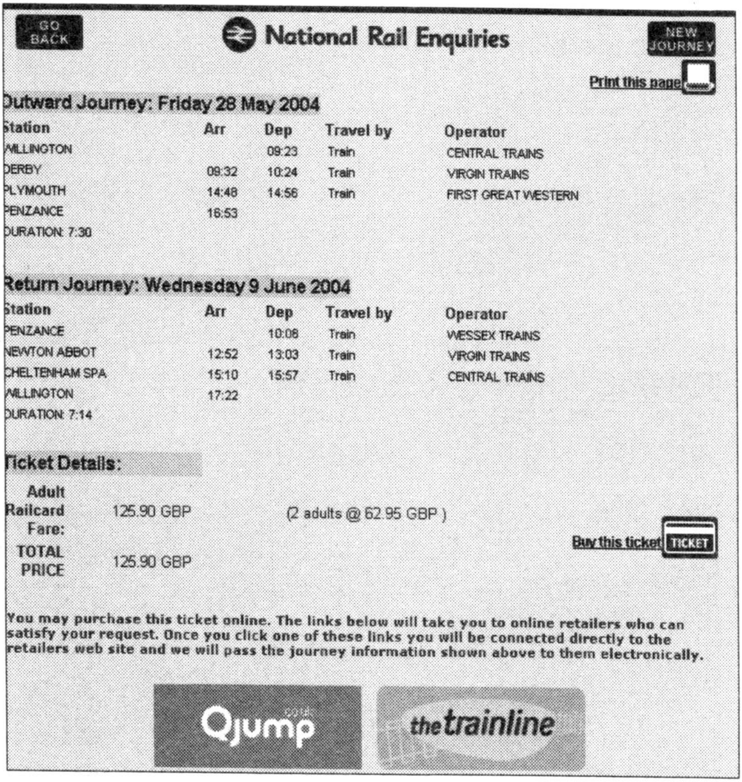

If you are happy with the details of the journey, you can click **TheTrainline** icon shown above, to purchase your tickets online. Alternatively there is a telephone icon at the bottom of the page which lists the numbers to use for ordering tickets by telephone.

Travelling Further Afield by Train

The Man in Seat Sixty-One is an incredible Web site and is the work of just one man, Mark Smith. The site provides information about trains all over the world, including times and prices and very much more. Although the Web site does not provide its own online booking facilities, there are links to specialist online booking agencies. As Mark Smith says, he just hopes to "cover the cost of hosting the Web site and buy a beer or two". The site is packed with all sorts of interesting and unusual information about global rail travel, such as how to travel from London to Vietnam by train - should you ever feel the desire. **The Man in Seat Sixty-One** is well worth a visit at:

www.seat61.com

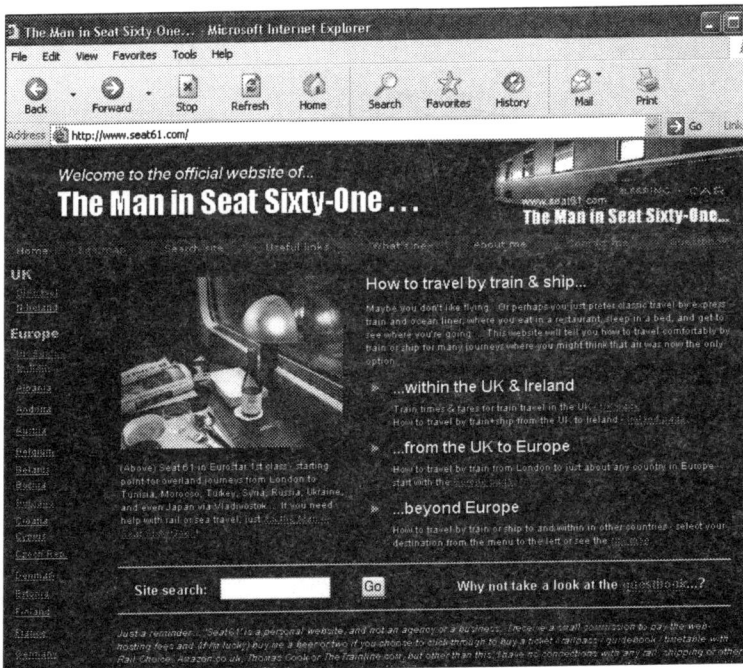

Rail Travel Web Sites

National Rail

This is the Web site administered by The Association of Train Operating Companies (ATOC) and provides links to all of the main sources of rail information.

www.nationalrail.co.uk

TheTrainline

Timetables and online booking for rail travel across UK and Europe, also links to flights, car hire, hotels and Eurostar service.

www.thetrainline.com

Rail Europe

Travel to Europe by Eurostar, high-speed rail travel including car transport by French Motorail service.

www.raileurope.co.uk

European Rail

UK based rail travel agency specializing in travel to Europe, including timetables, prices, online booking.

www.europeanrail.com

Eurotunnel

Online passenger bookings for crossing of the channel.

www.eurotunnel.com

Eurostar

High-speed rail service linking London, Paris, Brussels, Amsterdam, Bruges and other European destinations.

www.eurostar.com

World Wide Rail Operators

The Travel Bureau

Online booking of rail passes for USA, Australia and New Zealand, as well as Europe.

www.usa-by-rail.com

Amtrak

This is a major American train operator offering route planning, a virtual tour of trains and sleeping arrangements, online booking and links to all main travel and holiday services.

www.amtrak.com

Far East & China Rail Train Tour

Escorted train tours to China, Taiwan, Korea and East Asia.

www.chinarail.travel.com

The Orient Express

This famous company provides luxury rail tours and holidays through UK, Europe, Asia and Australia and has hotels all over the world.

www.orient-express.com

Japan Rail Pass

The Japan Rail Pass allows tourists on short-stay sightseeing visits to travel almost anywhere in the country.

www.japanrailpass.net

Man in Seat Sixty-One

As discussed earlier, this incredible site is one man's work to provide global information on rail travel and related travel subjects.

www.seat61.com

Scenic Railways in the UK

There are lots of scenic railways in the Britain, many of which had fallen into disrepair until being restored in recent years by enthusiastic volunteers. These railways pass through some of the most spectacular countryside to be found in Britain. Web sites giving brief details of some of the most well-known scenic railways are listed on the next few pages. Enter the Web address into the **Address Bar** in Internet Explorer to find more details of the railways, such as opening times, prices, timetables, routes, stopping-off points and facilities for refreshments, etc.

Rheilffordd Ffestiniog Railway

This narrow-gauge steam railway was built to replace earlier horse-drawn wagons, carrying slate from the mines in the mountains at Blaenau Ffestiniog to the harbour at Porthmadog. This is a very spectacular route from the mountains down to the sea.

www.festrail.co.uk

'Prince' (built 1863)

FR Homepage
The Route
Trains this Week
Timetables 2004
Fares 2004
Y Cerdyn
Special Events 2004
Welsh Highland Rly.
FR History
Spooner's Cafe Bar
Locomotives
Rolling Stock
Guest Driving
Slate Shunt
FR Society
Volunteering
The Railway Shop
Media Contacts
FR Feedback Form
Photo Library

Vale of Rheidol Railway

This is one of the Great Little Trains of Wales. It was the last steam railway owned by British Rail until it was privatized in 1989. The railway was built to serve the lead mines of the Rheidol Valley. The narrow-gauge track (about 2 feet wide) runs a distance of nearly 12 miles from Aberystwyth to Devil's Bridge.

www.rheidolrailway.co.uk

The Snowdon Mountain Railway

This spectacular railway climbs Snowdon, the highest mountain in England and Wales, from Llanberis (353ft) to the Summit Station (3494ft). The narrow-gauge locomotives use a special rack and pinion system in which toothed cogwheels engage with the track, providing traction on the ascent and braking on the way down.

www.snowdonrailway.co.uk

Launceston Steam Railway

This narrow-gauge railway in Cornwall follows the valley of the River Kensey, linking Launceston with the hamlet of New Mills.

www.narrow-gauge-pleasure.co.uk

North Yorkshire Moors Railway

This is a full-size steam railway travelling 18 miles through the Yorkshire moors from the market town of Pickering to the village of Grosmont. There are lots of stopping-off points to enable keen walkers to explore the moors.

www.nymr.demon.co.uk

WELCOME ABOARD..

The North Yorkshire Moors Railway provides some 18 miles of preserved steam railway running through the spectacular scenery of the North Yorkshire Moors. The line is owned by the North Yorkshire Historical Railway Trust who have run the line as a living museum since 1974. The North Yorkshire Moors Railway is a great outdoor experience for all the family. Come and join the fun!

NYMR

NORTH YORKSHIRE MOORS RAILWAY

BUY TICKETS ON-LINE NOW

The Severn Valley Railway

This is a standard-gauge (i.e. full-size) steam railway running 16 miles from Kidderminster in Worcestershire to Bridgnorth in Shropshire.

www.svr.co.uk

The Settle-Carlisle Railway

This is part of the National Rail network with a regular scheduled service. Considered to be one of Britain's most spectacular rail journeys, the route of 72 miles goes from Settle in the Yorkshire Dales to Carlisle in Cumbria.

www.settle-carlisle.co.uk

Arranging a Flight

Introduction

There has been an increase in cheap air travel in recent years, particularly in Europe, with the arrival of low-cost airlines such as easyJet, Ryanair, FlyBE and bmibaby. The Internet is a major factor in this flourishing business, with online booking facilities, last-minute deals and special offers. A major advantage is that you can make all of your travel and holiday arrangements online, often from one Web site, or *portal,* with links to all of the services such as flights, accommodation, car hire and travel insurance.

Some special offers with the low-cost operators provide flights into Europe for under £20 and in general you may be able to buy tickets for under £100 on a regular basis.

The Internet gives you access to hundreds of airlines throughout the world. Such is the central role of the Internet in attracting business and selling flights that increasingly some airlines are referred to by their Web address, for example **bmibaby.com**, **flybe.com** and **easyJet.com**. Passengers booking with easyJet, for example, receive discounts for booking online and some special promotions may be exclusive to Internet customers.

Searching for a Flight

If you arrange a holiday through a traditional High Street travel agent, perhaps after seeing an advert in a newspaper, the flight arrangements will be part of the package. However, the Internet really comes into its own when you are arranging your own flight. As always a search engine such as Google can be relied on to deliver the required information. Another approach is to use one of the online travel Web sites such as **expedia.co.uk**, **ebookers.com**, **uk.travel.yahoo.com** or **cheapflights.co.uk**.

Suppose you wanted to find an economical flight to Venice from a convenient local airport near your home, East Midlands for example.

The keywords **flight east midlands venice** were entered into Google (**www.google.co.uk**), as shown below. (Searching with Google was described in detail in Chapter 3).

Google quickly responded with the following link, near the top of the list of search results.

As can be seen above, this search result is a link to the Cheapflights.co.uk Web site, shown on the next page.

www.cheapflights.co.uk

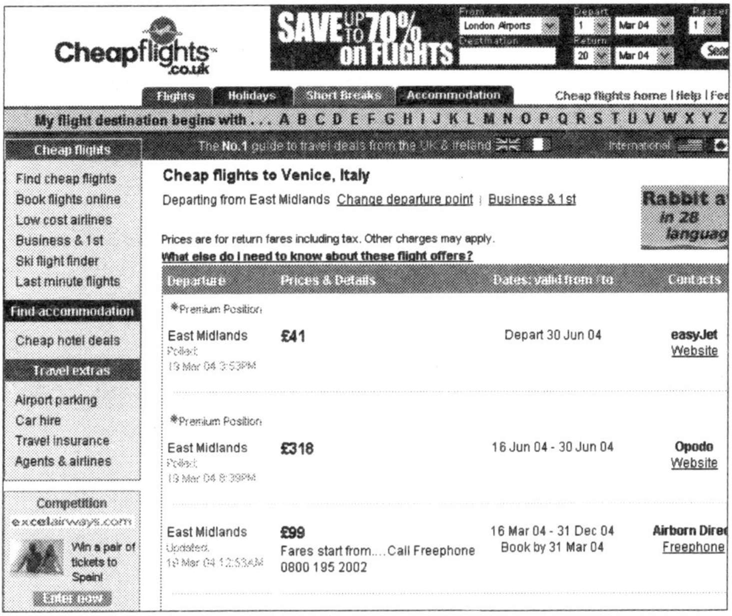

On the above extract from the Cheapflights.co.uk Web site, the **easyJet** flight to Venice appears at the top. Cheapflights.co.uk is "a neutral advertising platform showing viewers a large number of competitive deals...". The Cheapflights.co.uk site doesn't allow you to make the actual booking; to book online you have to click the link to your chosen airline.

The links to the airlines are shown down the right-hand side of the above Web page. Clicking the **easyJet** link shown on the right, for example, opens up their Web site, as shown on the next page.

book online step 12345

To check availability and fares, simply tell us where you want to fly and when.

from

Edinburgh (EDI)
East Midlands (EMA)
Faro (FAO)
Geneva (GVA)

to

Glasgow (GLA)
Malaga (AGP)
Prague (PRG)
Venice Marco Polo (VCE)

flying out on

21 | March 2004

returning on

22 | March 2004

passengers

2 adults

We lower fares!
From London to: ONE WAY FROM

Bilbao   £6.99
Madrid   £16.99
Aberdeen   £6.99

Click for details...   (Taxes & charges excluded.)

FIVE brand new destinations   ...click here
Basel, Budapest, Dortmund Cologne/Bonn, and Ljubljana

quick answers
Enter keywords e.g. "baggage allowance"

go

route information
We offer 148 routes between 44 key European airports across the UK, France, Spain, Switzerland, the Netherlands, Denmark, Italy, Czech Republic, Greece, Germany, Portugal, Hungary and Slovenia. destinations | timetables

Changing your booking?

On the easyJet Web site you select the airports for your departure and destination, the dates of your flights and the number of passengers. Click the **show prices** button and a screen appears quoting the total price for your chosen flights and also prices for travelling on alternative days. You then select from these various flights and proceed to make a booking. The online booking form requires you to enter your name, home address and e-mail address (for confirmation of your booking). Finally enter your credit card details to make the payment.

Security

As discussed later in this book, all financial transactions are carried out using a *secure server*, preventing third parties from intercepting the data as it travels between your computer and the airline's Web server computer.

Air Travel Portals

Many Web sites provide a complete travel service, including online flight bookings, hotels and car hire. These are known as *portals* and act as gateways, directing you through links to the entire range of travel services. You can see some of the major travel portals by simply typing **travel** into the Google search engine, as described previously.

Google responds with a list of the search results, showing several of the major travel portals at the top of the page.

Although only the single word **travel** was entered into Google, you can see that air travel figures strongly in the results. You can also see above that these portals allow airline tickets, hotel rooms, car rental, cruises and holidays to be booked online.

Cheapflights.co.uk

Clicking on the **Travel** link shown on the right (and also shown on the right of the search results on the

previous page) opens up the Web page shown below.

www.cheapflights.co.uk

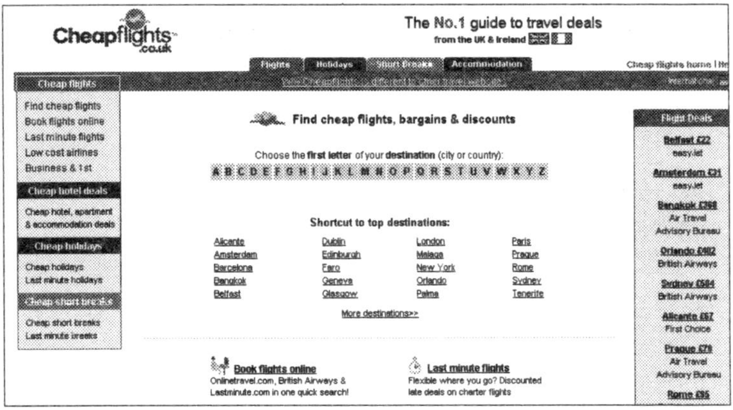

In the centre of the screen there are links to top city destinations, or alternatively you can click the first letter of your destination's name. For example, if you want to book a flight to **Dublin**, select this city from the destinations in the centre of the screen.

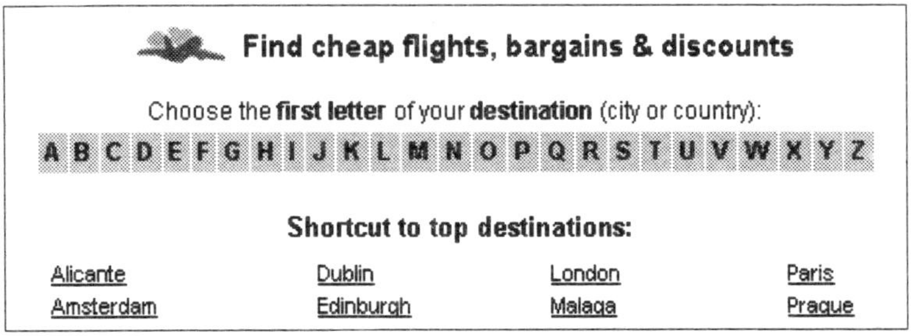

The Cheapflights.co.uk web site then presents a list of airports in Britain, operating flights to Dublin. The number of flights per day from a given airport is shown in brackets after the airport name, as shown below.

For example, there are 9 fights a day to Dublin from East Midlands. Click the name of your departure airport to see a list of flights with different airlines, as shown below

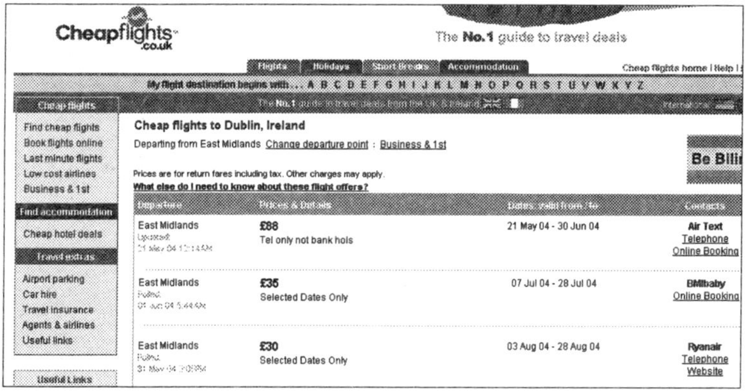

When you have chosen a flight, click the airline or company link on the right to make the online booking.

At the top left of the Cheapflights.co.uk screen is a set of links giving various methods of finding the cheapest flight to a given destination. The link **Find cheap flights** shown on the right presents a list of destinations and then you select the airport for your departure. From a particular airport you

Cheap flights
Find cheap flights
Book flights online
Last minute flights
Low cost airlines
Business & 1st

can see the available flights and, if suitable, make an online booking, as discussed previously.

The link **Book flights online** feature shown above on the Cheapflights.co.uk Web site leads to a search facility based on **onlinetravel.com, British Airways** and **lastminute.com**.

Here you enter details such as your departure airport and destination, ticket type, departure and return dates and the details of the people in your party. Click on any of the three links shown on the right above under **Search using** to find available flights and, if desired, make an online booking.

Clicking on the **Last minute flights** link shown at the top of the previous page allows you to take advantage of cheap charter flights leaving within 30 days to a variety of destinations and for a fixed number of nights' duration.

⏱ **Last minute flights**

Flexible where you go? Get great last minute flight discounts leaving in the next 30 days:

Please note: The following are mostly discounted charter flights with a fixed number of nights duration

Click on the date on which you want to travel:

June 2004							July 2004						
Mon	Tue	Wed	Thu	Fri	Sat	Sun	Mon	Tue	Wed	Thu	Fri	Sat	Sun
	1	2	3	4	5	6				1	2	3	4
7	8	9	10	11	12	13	5	6	7	8	9	10	11
14	15	16	17	18	19	20	12	13	14	15	16	17	18
21	22	23	24	25	26	27	19	20	21	22	23	24	25
28	29	30					26	27	28	29	30	31	

The **Low cost airlines** link on the previous page presents a list of airports and lists special deals to various destinations, available on specific dates in the future. The extract from the Cheapflights.co.uk Web site below shows flights from East Midlands and Edinburgh, for example. If you click the small hotel icon to the left of the destination name, sites are displayed which list accommodation in the chosen city.

East Midlands

From	To	Fare	Dates	Airline
East Midlands	🏨 Cologne	£30	Aug 03 - 25	easyJet
	🏨 Venice Marco Polo	£65	Aug 10 - 11	easyJet
	🏨 Faro	£112	Jul 06 - 07	easyJet
	🏨 Malaga	£120	Jul 06 - 07	easyJet
	🏨 Alicante	£135	Jul 06 - 13	easyJet
	🏨 Amsterdam	£39	Jun 09 - 30	bmibaby
	🏨 Prague	£59	Jun 09 - 29	bmibaby
	🏨 Murcia	£133	Oct 02 - 16	bmibaby

Edinburgh

From	To	Fare	Dates	Airline
Edinburgh	🏨 Dublin	£50	Aug 17 - 31	Aer Lingus
	🏨 Paris	£98	Sep 04 - 29	British Airways
	🏨 Paris CDG	£98	Sep 04 - 29	British Airways
	🏨 Madrid	£134	Dec 01 - 29	British Airways
	🏨 Amsterdam	£60	Aug 11 - 18	easyJet

Flight Deals

Belfast £22
easyJet

Amsterdam £31
easyJet

Bangkok £368
Air Travel
Advisory Bureau

On the right of the Cheapflights.co.uk screen are **Flight Deals** as shown in the extract on the left. Clicking on any of these links leads to a list of special prices with different airlines for journeys to a particular destination. Please note that these prices may only apply on certain departure dates.

Cheap hotel deals

Cheap hotel, apartment & accommodation deals

Cheap holidays

Cheap holidays
Last minute holidays

Cheap short breaks

Cheap short breaks
Last minute breaks

On the left of the Cheapflights.co.uk screenshot shown on page 110 are links to hotels and accommodation and also holidays and short breaks.

Useful links shown below on the left presents a list of further links leading to information on a wide variety of subjects helpful to the traveller. **Useful currency links** displays various currency converters plus Visa and Master card locaters for "hole-in-the wall" machines. **Disabled Traveller** shown below provides links to a list of Web sites designed to help people with special needs. Many of these sites are mentioned elsewhere in this book. **Home Exchanges** helps you to swap homes with people in different parts of the world, for a holiday. **Preparations** assists with planning a trip or holiday and obtaining worldwide weather forecasts.

Travel extras		
Airport parking	Cheapflights-ology	Trains and public transport
Car hire	Consumer rights	Travel company regulators
Travel insurance	Disabled traveller	Travel guides
Agents & airlines	Ecotourism	Travel warnings
Useful links	Family travel	Useful currency links
	Flight tracker	Visas and passports
	Glossary of flying terms	Volunteering
	Home exchanges	Weather - now

CenNet

This is a Web site presenting "Lifestyles for Today's Over 50's". Apart from travel, a wide range of other subjects are also covered such as **Your Money** and **Home & Garden**. An extract from the **Travel** page is shown below. There are links to every type of holiday such as short breaks, singles and self-catering.

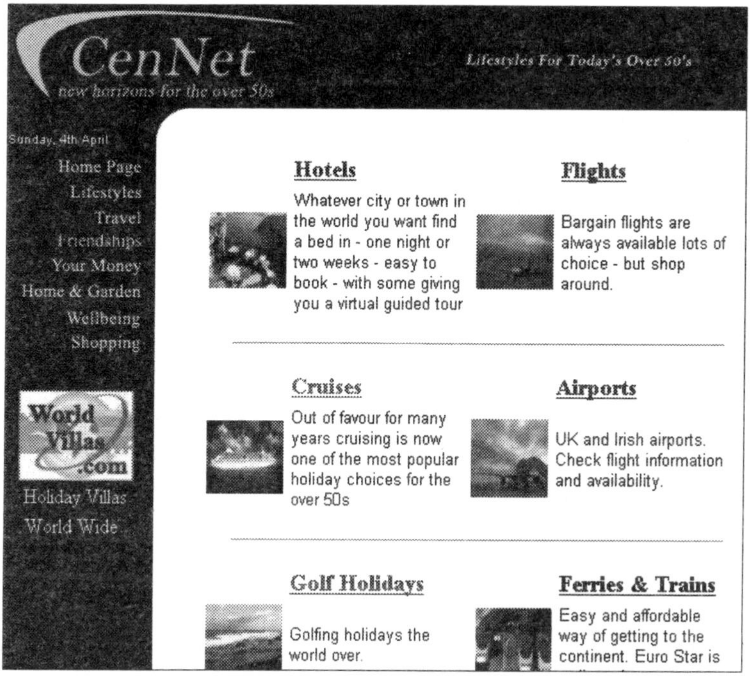

Clicking **Flights**, shown above, leads to the Web sites of many of the leading airlines and online travel companies, such as Expedia and e-bookers. The **Airports** link above allows you to check the latest flight information at many of the major airports in the UK.

www.cennet.co.uk

The CenNet site on the previous page has a link to **Travel 55**, a Web site offering discounts of 5-10% on travel and holidays, many of which are biased towards the older generation. The **Travel 55** web site includes an online membership form.

www.travel55.co.uk/club.html

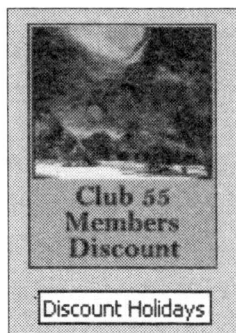

Club 55
Members
Discount

Discount Holidays

The Travel 55 site also offers discounts with **Leger Holidays**, who have coach tours to a comprehensive choice of short city breaks and longer holidays in the UK, Europe and America. Many of these will be of interest to older travellers, including battlefield tours, Christmas Markets, flower shows, horse racing, rail holidays and cruises as well as relaxing holidays in most popular destinations.

Leger Holidays
Leger Holidays Special Offers For Travel 55

Return To Home Page

All of the Leger Holidays & Tours featured here are discounted from the brochure prices.

Holidays by Coach, Air & Rail

For more information about each holiday please click on the link.

When booking with Leger Holidays please quote our Ref: T5501 to ensure your discount.

Tel Leger Reservations on 0845 458 5604. Open

All of these Leger Holidays & Short Breaks have been discounted from the brochure prices.
Travel by Coach, Rail or Fly.
Group Travel Available. Contact us for details.

Battlefields Tours
WWI , WWII & Colonial Wars. Battlefield tours Europe & Worldwide. Specialist Battlefield Guides.
View

Disneyland® Resort Paris
Join the magic at Christmas, New Year and summer 2004 at Disneyland® Paris. Coach, Air, Eurostar or Self Drive.
View

Holidays Italy
Holidays throughout Italy. Short breaks or longer holidays. Travel by coach, rail or take a plane.
View

Christmas Markets
2004 Christmas Markets
A superb selection of European Christmas markets. Christmas shopping with a difference.
View

ebookers.com

Some Web sites, such as **ebookers.com**, allow you to arrange your travel insurance online. For example, open up the Web site at **www.ebookers.com** and click the **Insurance** link along the top of the screen. This displays insurance rates for various destinations and periods of cover.

You are advised above to print out a copy of the insurance policy. This can be done by clicking on the link **Insurance policy** shown in the lower centre above. The premiums listed in this example are for persons aged 16-64 years. For anyone aged 65-74 years, the premiums are double those in the above table; anyone over 75 years of age is given a telephone number to call for a quote.

There are also **Multi-Trip Policies** for anyone who travels several times a year. Not surprisingly, different rates apply for **Ski Insurance**, accessed by the button shown above.

If you wish to proceed with the insurance, click the **Buy a Policy** button towards the bottom left of the screen shown on the previous page. You are required to select your destination from **Europe**, **Australia & New Zealand** or **Worldwide**. Then enter full details of the members of your party, dates of travel and your credit card to complete the transaction. Security issues relating to Internet financial transactions are discussed later in this book.

If you're not familiar with the latest travel procedures, the **ebookers.com** Web site includes a useful **Travellers checklist**. This includes information on **Passports & Visas**, advice on credit cards and local currency and precautions for staying healthy. There is also advice for those taking medication, the need to pack prescriptions and the form E111 to claim for free emergency medical care in Europe.

Security in airports is very strict nowadays; apart from the usual passport checks, you and your hand luggage will be scanned and subjected to a thorough search if anything suspicious is detected. The following is an extract from the **Travellers' checklist** on the **ebookers.com** Web site.

At the airport – hand luggage

Airport security has increased and there are certain precautions we advise you with revised rules and regulations. It is important that you don't pack any of the f luggage under any circumstances:s

Toy/replica guns (metal or plastic)
Catapults
Household cutlery
Knives with blades of any length
Razor blade
Tools
Scissors
Tweezers
Hypodermic needles (unless required for medical reasons)
Knitting needles

Airline Passengers with Special Needs

If you have a disability or serious illness you should contact your chosen airline well in advance of your departure date. Depending on the particular impairment you may need to obtain medical clearance to travel; or the airline may need to make special arrangements for you.

The Allgohere Web site shown below includes a directory of all of the main airlines in the world. For each airline there is a summary of their policy towards disabled passengers. For example, some airlines will only carry wheelchairs if they are powered by dry cell batteries. (Wet cell batteries present a risk of dangerous acid spillage).

Some long-haul operators provide narrow aisle wheelchairs on larger aircraft and also wheelchair accessible toilets. There are also different policies towards guide dogs and the need for disabled passengers to be accompanied by a helper. Passengers with impaired vision may request large print or Braille versions of emergency procedures.

www.allgohere.com

ALL GO
HERE

incorporating

EVERYBODY
.co.uk

* Find hotels/services by UK County or Location * UK Hotel Central Res. Info * Airlines
* List/Advertise * About/How to Use * Symbols & Hotel Pricing Explained * Contact Us * Buy * News * Links

THE ALLGOHERE AIRLINE DIRECTORY.

SeniorJet Airlines

Reservations:	Administration:	Fares:	Fax:

Medical clearance not usually required unless health risk. Will carry manual wheelchairs/electric wheelchairs with dry or wet cell batteries in hold. Passenger with disability advised to travel accompanied. Guide dogs allowed on domestic flights/not allowed on international flights. Oxygen can be provided given advance notice. Stretchers can be carried on larger aircrafts. Aircrafts have standard on-board toilets. Can cater for special dietary requirements. Where available, air-bridge usually used for boarding otherwise lifting vehicle used if necessary. Wheelchair users may not be able to fly on smaller aircrafts. Discounts may be available for blind passengers and their companion on certain domestic flights. Narrow isle wheelchairs available on larger aircrafts on long haul flights. Emergency procedures available in Braille or large print by request on some flights, but where not available, on boarding cabin staff will advise passengers on a one to one basis. All non domestic flights have at least one member of cabin crew who has disability training. Introducing Medlink heart monitors on all long haul flights allowing cabin crew to provide better assistance in cases of heart problems in mid flight by being able to supply doctors on the ground with directly updated "real time" analysis of a passenger's condition.

Airline Policies and Regulations

An airline's main Web site should contain an outline of their policies towards passengers. This includes the amount of luggage, hand baggage and any excess baggage charges. Items which must not be carried in hand baggage, such as knives, scissors and snooker cues should also be listed. Bicycles, skis and golf clubs may be carried free of charge but there may be an additional charge for items such as hang-gliders, surfboards and firearms. The airline's web site should also outline the policy towards disabled passengers and give advice on health issues such as steps to reduce the risk of Deep Vein Thrombosis (DVT).

You should also be informed of the airline's policy on refunds and cancellations. Passengers must normally check in at least 30 minutes or more before the scheduled departure time although longer is recommended and may be essential for passengers with special needs. Photographic ID is required at check-in for all flights including domestic routes such as the following extract from the easyJet Web site.

Acceptable forms of ID on UK domestic flights are:

- A valid passport – an expired passport can be used up to a maximum of two years after expiry
- Valid photographic EU or Swiss national identity card
- Valid photographic driving licence
- Valid armed forces identity card
- Valid police warrant card/badge
- Valid airport employees security identity pass
- A child on parent' s passport is an acceptable form of ID
- CitizenCard
- Valid photographic firearm certificate
- Valid Government-issued identity card

Air Travel Web Sites

The next few pages give addresses of many popular travel companies and airlines. Simply type the address of each Web site into the **Address** bar of the Internet Explorer.

Expedia.co.uk

As described earlier, Expedia is a large Internet travel agent offering online access to flights and related services.

www.expedia.co.uk

Opodo UK

This is an online travel service backed by some of the world's major airlines. Opodo offers a complete range of flight and related services.

www.pastplaces.com/opodo.asp

ebookers.com

In addition to online booking of flights and holidays worldwide, this company provides general holiday information, train and ferry tickets and booking of cruises.

www.ebookers.com

Travelocity

This is a major online travel agency giving good facilities to search for flights, hotels, holidays and most other travel requirements. (**.com** is the American Web site).

www.travelocity.co.uk   **www.travelocity.com**

This is Travel

Apart from comprehensive flight and holiday information, this site has many other useful Web pages including a travel checklist, advice on passports and visas and an **Over 55s** channel with articles and ideas for holidays.

www.thisistravel.co.uk

Cheapflights.co.uk

This is a travel site specializing in cheap flights, bargains and discounts, to worldwide destinations.

www.cheapflights.co.uk

CenNet

This is a lifestyle Web site, described earlier, for the over 50s and includes a travel section with links to major airlines.

www.cennet.co.uk

Saga Holidays

Saga offers a wide range of over-50s holidays in the UK, Europe and worldwide. Saga Travel Insurance is designed specifically for the over 50s. Foreign currency can be ordered online and delivered to your home or the airport.

www.saga.co.uk

deckchair.com

This is a Web site founded by Sir Bob Geldof and specialises in city breaks and holidays in Europe, the Caribbean, USA, Canada and South Africa, etc.

www.deckchair.com

lastminute.com

One of the original ".com" companies, **lastminute.com** offers special late deals on flights, holidays (including short breaks to Europe's top cities), restaurant meals and days out in the UK. This is a very versatile Web site offering all sorts of competitive deals on a wide range of services, in addition to comprehensive travel and holiday offers.

www.lastminute.com

British Airways - ba.com

The long established British flagship airline offers worldwide service, including different classes of seat, such as the **Executive Club** for frequent business travellers. The Web site contains a wealth of helpful information in addition to basic flight details, including notes on in-flight medical issues and the airline's provision of help for disabled passengers and those with special needs.

www.britishairways.com

easyJet.com

A leading low-cost airline offering 152 routes between 44 European airports, with Web site links to all major travel services - hotels, car rental, travel insurance, etc.

www.easyjet.com

Ryanair

Ryanair is another prominent low-cost airline offering flights around Europe, especially to Ireland, with some very cheap special offers. Also provides services such as Ryanair Travel Insurance and the Ryanair Credit Card.

www.ryanair.com

bmi

Otherwise known as British Midland International, this company provides cheap flights on both transatlantic and European routes.

www.flybmi.com

bmibaby.com

"The airline with tiny fares" is the low-cost arm of **bmi**, operating from the UK to various European destinations.

bmibabyextras.com provides links to all of the related travel services - hotels, insurance, car rental, etc.

www.bmibaby.com

skytrax

This Web site surveys airline passengers' opinions and produces star rankings, such as the 4-star report on British Airways, shown below. All the world's airlines and airports are covered and ratings include assessments of the cabin crew and airport services.

www.airlinequality.com

Yahoo!

Yahoo! is a well-known search engine and also has a directory system including a listing of all of the world's most popular airlines. To open the list of airlines, enter **www.dir.yahoo.com** into the **Address** bar then navigate through the various sub-directories, until you reach the **Airlines** directory as shown below in the line:

Directory > Business and Economy > Shopping and Services > Travel and Transportation > Airlines.

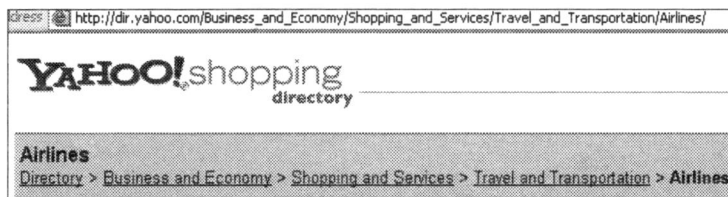

Clicking the name of an airline (shown underlined below) opens up the airline's own Web site.

Airlines of the Web

This is an interesting Web site, providing a listing of 500 of the world's leading airlines.

www.flyaow.com

To find an airline's Web site, click the **airlines** link and a map of the world is presented; click the required country on the map, then select the airline from the resulting list to open up the airline's web site.

Airlines of the Web also offers a special **Cyberfares** feature, providing discounted tickets and last-minute offers only available to online customers.

Another link, **Air Tips**, provides advice on many aspects of air travel, including airline rules and healthy flying.

The **Air Tips** page also has a link, **All Go Here**, a guide to disability-friendly airlines and hotels, also discussed on page119.

ALL GO HERE
incorporating
EVERYBODY .co.uk

The directory of UK hotels and other hospitality related services which are all disability-friendly so can be used by disabled or able bodied people

The world's ONLY accessible airline guide & the UK's most popular directory of disability-friendly hotels.

www.allgohere.com   **www.everybody.co.uk**

8

Arranging Accommodation

Introduction

If you are booking a complete holiday package through a travel agent then your hotel will normally be arranged as part of the deal. This chapter shows how you can find and book your own accommodation online. The Internet can help you find every conceivable type of accommodation to suit any size of budget.

You'll probably know where you want to go; for example, you may have always wanted to see a particular city or part of the world. You might need to visit somewhere for a special event such as a wedding, anniversary, sports meeting or sightseeing attraction. Or you may just want to take off for a short break on the spur of the moment. This chapter looks at several different types of trip and shows how the Internet can be used to arrange suitable accommodation. The examples are:

- Camping and caravanning in the UK or Europe.
- Self-catering in a cottage in Cornwall.
- Bed and breakfast in Northumberland.
- A holiday in Venice.

Camping and Caravanning

You might start by entering the keywords **camping** and **caravanning** into Google. (Capital letters and words like **and** are ignored). The search results display links to various camp sites including the one in North Wales, shown below.

www.croeso-cynnes-wales.co.uk/acc/camping.html

Map	Name	Grade	Facilities	Phone	
(7)	Gwern Gof Isaf			01690 720276	more info
(3)	Rynys Farm Camping Site			01690 710218	more info
(2)	Bodnant Caravan Park	★★★★		01492 640248	more info
(1)	Barcdy Caravan Park	★★★★		01766 770736	more info
(8)	Tyn y Wern			01490 460419	more info
(5)	Pant Glas Canol			01824 710639	more info
(6)	Pen Llan			01492 640591	more info
(4)	Llwyn Richard			01492 640368	more info

Symbol Key

- Tents taken
- Dormobiles taken
- Touring caravans taken
- Static caravans available

As shown above, there is a key showing the type of camping available - tents, Dormobiles, touring caravans and static caravans. You can obtain more details of a particular site, as shown below, by clicking a point on the location map shown above or by clicking one of the **more info** links.

Campsite • Gwersyll

Gwern Gôf Isaf Farm
Capel Curig
Betws-y-Coed
Snowdonia
North Wales
LL24 0EU

Phone : 01690 720276
Website : www.gwerngofisaf.co.uk
Dafydd & Elizabeth Williams

Please mention 'Croeso Cynnes' when phoning

Gwern Gôf Isaf is beautifully situated on a traditional hill-farm between Capel Curig and Llyn Ogwen, close to the base of the well-known peak of Tryfan. Set in the heart of the mountains it is ideally situated for walking or climbing the surrounding peak of the Glyders, and the Carneddau. This site is popular with families, groups, and individuals. There is also a bunkhouse.

A Google search for **camping** and **caravanning** finds a lot of other useful Web sites, as listed below.

UKWEBFIND

This site has links to holiday parks throughout the United Kingdom, including a large number of campsites in Wales.

www.ukwebfind.co.uk

The Caravanning Site

This is a directory of touring parks throughout the UK, Ireland and America. Sites are listed in each area, with links leading to photographs and descriptions of the facilities at individual sites. USA fly-drive holidays are also advertised with descriptions of camp sites in various states.

www.thecaravanningsite.co.uk

The Camping and Caravanning Club

This club has a complete range of support services for campers and caravanners, including insurance for caravans, tents and motor caravans. There is a breakdown recovery service, weather forecasting, guides to 3,500 sites in the UK and courses on safe towing. The Camping and Caravanning club offers special rates to members over 55 years of age.

www.campingandcaravanningclub.co.uk

Silver Surfers

The Silver Surfers web site has links to all sorts of services for older people, including a **Travel** section which includes a sub-section on **Camping, Caravanning & Motorhomes**. There are links to numerous camping-related Web sites in the UK and Europe, including **ukcampsite.com** and **caravan-sitefinder.co.uk**.

www.silversurfers.net/travel-camping.html

Travel World

This Web site has links to a large number of camp sites in the UK and Europe, including the award-winning Canvas Holidays, shown below.

travel.world.co.uk/camping.htm

Canvas Holidays — Europe's finest mobile home and camping holidays

home | your holiday | find a holiday | about us | special offers | help & advice

find a holiday ▸

find accommodation ▸

early summer sun for less... save up to 40% ▸

Welcome to Canvas 2004

We are an independent family camping holiday company with 39 years experience of providing self-drive camping and mobile home holidays in France and the rest of Europe, including Spain, Italy, Luxembourg, Germany, Austria, Switzerland and Holland.

A Canvas Holiday is a package camping holiday with a difference. With complete flexibility on dates, duration and travel arrangements, your holiday is tailored to suit you.

The UK Camp Site

This site allows you look at camp sites all over the UK and Europe, by clicking on county names or areas on a map. The facilities at each site are listed and there are reviews of some of the sites by campers, describing their experiences. There is also a **Message Board** allowing campers to chat to other enthusiasts, share tips and ask for advice. Another page on the Web site allows members to place free advertisements for tents, caravans and other camping equipment, either wanted or for sale.

www.ukcampsite.co.uk

A Country Cottage in Cornwall

If you prefer self-catering holidays, then the Internet can provide access to thousands of properties in all parts of the United Kingdom. Searching for country cottages using Google produces the following list of links to Web sites.

Most of the results at the top of the list are agencies operating online databases of cottage properties. On the right is a link to **Classic Cottages.** This is a particularly attractive Web site which has many advantages compared with the traditional brochure sent out through the conventional post. These advantages include online availability checks and also prices and other information which should always be up-to-date. A **Special Offers** feature on the **Classic Cottages** site lists properties at reduced rents. These may be available because of cancellations, for example. You can also carry out a search for a suitable property after completing a detailed list of your requirements, as shown on the next page.

www.classiccottages.co.uk

First you enter the dates you wish to start and end your holiday and the duration in weeks. You must also specify the number of adults, children and pets in your party.

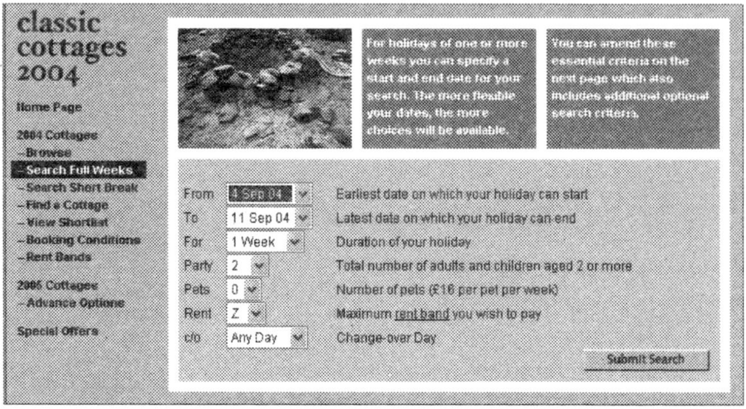

The **Rent** is entered as a letter representing the maximum you want to pay. These letters and the corresponding prices at different times of the year are given on a table viewed by clicking the **Rent Bands** link on the left of the screen.

If you now click the **Submit Search** button at the bottom right of the screen shown above, a map of the South West of England appears showing the number of properties available in various areas. On this screen you can enter more detailed requirements, such as distance from a town or having sea views, open fires and no smoking.

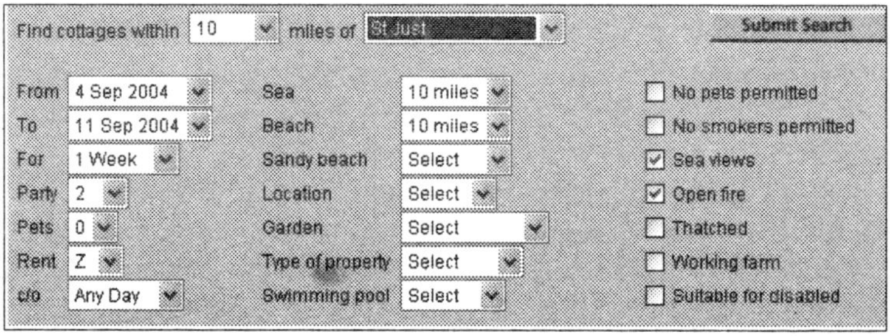

When you submit this more detailed search the results are displayed down the right-hand side of the screen as shown below. The number of cottages matching the search criteria is listed in each area of the West Country. For example, two suitable cottages were found in South West Cornwall.

Search Results	Totals
The West Country	9
Cornwall	7
– Far West	2
– South West	2
– North Coast	0
– Between the Moors	0
– South Coast	3
Devon	2
– North Devon	1
– Dartmoor	0
– South Devon	1
Somerset	0
Dorset	0

Click on the map or links on the right to view listings   Switch Map View

Find cottages within [10 ▼] miles of [St Just ▼]   Submit Search

From	4 Sep 2004 ▼	Sea	10 miles ▼	☐ No pets permitted
To	11 Sep 2004 ▼	Beach	10 miles ▼	☐ No smokers permitted
For	1 Week ▼	Sandy beach	Select ▼	☑ Sea views
Party	2 ▼	Location	Select ▼	☑ Open fire
Pets	0 ▼	Garden	Select ▼	☐ Thatched
Rent	Z ▼	Type of property	Select ▼	☐ Working farm
c/o	Any Day ▼	Swimming pool	Select ▼	☐ Suitable for disabled

If you allow the cursor to hover over a region in the list, the corresponding area on the map is highlighted. If you click the **Switch Map View** button, the map is redrawn with all of the available properties marked as small squares. Allowing the cursor to hover over a square displays brief details of the property, as shown on the right.

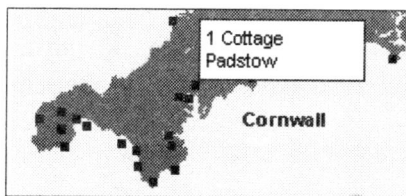

1 Cottage
Padstow

Cornwall

If you click an entry in the list such as **South West**, the cottages available in that area are listed with a thumbnail, i.e. miniature, picture. Now click the thumbnail or the link word **Description** to view full details and photographs of each cottage.

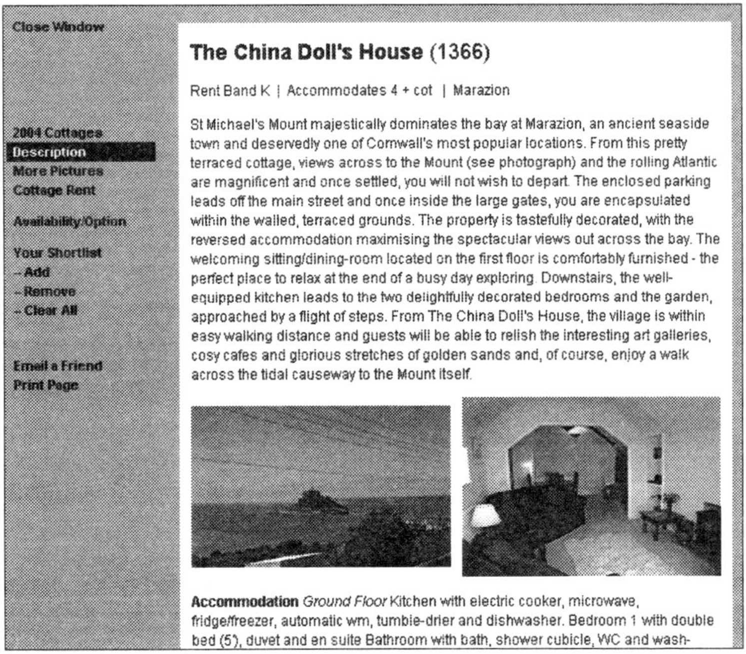

Close Window

2004 Cottages
Description
More Pictures
Cottage Rent

Availability/Option

Your Shortlist
- Add
- Remove
- Clear All

Email a Friend
Print Page

The China Doll's House (1366)

Rent Band K | Accommodates 4 + cot | Marazion

St Michael's Mount majestically dominates the bay at Marazion, an ancient seaside town and deservedly one of Cornwall's most popular locations. From this pretty terraced cottage, views across to the Mount (see photograph) and the rolling Atlantic are magnificent and once settled, you will not wish to depart. The enclosed parking leads off the main street and once inside the large gates, you are encapsulated within the walled, terraced grounds. The property is tastefully decorated, with the reversed accommodation maximising the spectacular views out across the bay. The welcoming sitting/dining-room located on the first floor is comfortably furnished - the perfect place to relax at the end of a busy day exploring. Downstairs, the well-equipped kitchen leads to the two delightfully decorated bedrooms and the garden, approached by a flight of steps. From The China Doll's House, the village is within easy walking distance and guests will be able to relish the interesting art galleries, cosy cafes and glorious stretches of golden sands and, of course, enjoy a walk across the tidal causeway to the Mount itself.

Accommodation *Ground Floor* Kitchen with electric cooker, microwave, fridge/freezer, automatic wm, tumble-drier and dishwasher. Bedroom 1 with double bed (5'), duvet and en suite Bathroom with bath, shower cubicle, WC and wash-

On the left-hand side of the **Classic Cottages** screen shown above, a link **Availability/Option** presents a grid showing the weeks when the cottage is available, booked or reserved. If you want to take out an option on this cottage, enter the required dates and click **Get Option Form**. This allows you to enter all of your personal details, name, address, etc., and submit the form, online prior to completing the booking.

Bed and Breakfast in Northumberland

This example looks at the charming town of Alnwick in Northumberland, recently voted "The Best Place to Live in Britain" after a nationwide survey considering quality of life and the beauty of the surroundings. Northumberland is famous for its many castles and spectacular landscape, including the Cheviot Hills.

We could try a search using the key words **bed, breakfast, alnwick** (remembering again that capital letters and words like **and** and **in** are not necessary in Google.) Searching with Google is covered in detail in Chapter 3.

Google	Web Images Groups News **more »**
	bed breakfast alnwick [Search]
	Search: ○ the web ⦿ pages from the UK

This search yields a great deal of accommodation, including individual hotels and guest houses as well as agencies providing accommodation all over the UK.

However, if you prefer the smaller type of bed and breakfast accommodation, you might want to exclude hotels from the list of search results. This can be achieved by using the minus sign (-), as in **-hotels**, shown below.

bed breakfast alnwick -hotels	Search

Finally, if you would like a more rural environment, then you could look for **farmhouse** accommodation as shown in the search criteria below.

bed breakfast alnwick -hotels farmhouse	Search

This search yields a useful 166 results for farmhouse bed and breakfast in the Alnwick area of Northumberland.

Web   Results **1 - 10** of about **166** for <u>bed</u> <u>breakfast</u> **alnwick** <u>-hotels</u> <u>farmhouse</u>

Bed & Breakfast Alnwick, Northumberland, B&B **Alnwick** Amble ...
... Click here to email. Click here for the Hipsburn **Farmhouse** Website. More B&B's, >>
Click here to view more **bed** & **breakfast's** in **Alnwick** or Northumberland. ...
www.**bed**and**breakfast**explorer.co.uk/counties/ north_east/fulldetail.asp?ID=175 - 18k -
Cached - Similar pages

  Bed & Breakfast Alnwick, B&B **Alnwick**
  ... Hipsburn **Farmhouse** is a spacious Georgian residence on a working farm, situated 0.5
  miles from Alnmouth. read more >>. **Bed & Breakfast** in **Alnwick**, ...
  www.**bed**and**breakfast**explorer.co.uk/ searchfield.asp?SValue=Alnwick&SType=+AND+ -
  19k - Cached - Similar pages
  [More results from www.bedandbreakfastexplorer.co.uk]

CORNHILLS **FARMHOUSE BED, BREAKFAST** & HOLIDAY COTTAGE
Bed & Breakfast at Cornhills ... Castles (Dunstanburgh, Bamburgh), Gardens (**Alnwick**,
Belsay, Wallington), walking along Hadrian's wall, fishing at Sweethope Lough ...
www.northumberland**farmhouse**.co.uk/ - 6k - 8 Apr 2004 - Cached - Similar pages

Bed & Breakfast, Alnwick, Morpeth, Northumberland, UK
Farmhouse bed and **breakfast** with en-suite rooms and evening meals by the River
Coquet near Morpeth and **Alnwick** in beautiful Northumberland, UK. ...
www.thistleyhaugh.co.uk/ - 4k - Cached - Similar pages

Northumberland **bed** and **breakfast** accommodation and self catering. ...
... Apartment, Northumberland B&B, Northumberland **Bed** and **Breakfast**, Northumberland
Cottage, Guest ... Farm House, Northumberland Inn, Northumberland **Farmhouse** ? ...
www.accommodationdata.com/England/Counties/northum.htm - 13k - Cached -
Similar pages

Dunns Houses **Farmhouse Bed** and **Breakfast** Otterburn Nr Newcastle ...
... The historic towns of Hexham, **Alnwick**, Morpeth, Newcastle, Hawick, Jedburgh,
Rothbury and Bellingham Village ~ all within easy access (Plenty of local Inns for ...
www.northumberlandfarmholidays.co.uk/tourist.html - 9k - Cached - Similar pages

---

Altogether there are 12 pages of results, all relevant to this particular search for accommodation. It's now just a case of clicking on each of the links to find some accommodation which appeals to you. Some of the search results are links to agencies which provide accommodation all over the United Kingdom. Other results take you to the Web site of an individual farmhouse, etc.

For example, Thistleyhaugh is a 685-acre working farm
providing bed and breakfast and has its own Web site.

www.thistleyhaugh.co.uk

Thistleyhaugh

Welcome   Sleeping   Dining   Sightseeing   Finding Us   Prices/Enquiries

Welcome

Thistleyhaugh is a picturesque Georgian farmhouse situated on the banks of the
River Coquet near Alnwick, Rothbury and Morpeth
in the heart of rural Northumberland.

Each of the Web pages has links to further pages, with
good-quality images of facilities such as bedrooms, the
dining room, local sightseeing and methods of contact.

Welcome   Sleeping   Dining   Sightseeing   Finding Us   Prices/Enquiries

Thistleyhaugh
Longhorsley, Morpeth
Northumberland, UK
NE65 8RG

Tel:
+44 (0)1665 570629

Email:
stay@thistleyhaugh.co.uk

Web Design by Snowgoose and Kimmerston Design

The accommodation is booked by completing the online enquiry form shown below, which can also be printed. This is then e-mailed to the establishment and the booking is completed by e-mail or telephone. There is also a section on the bottom of the form (not shown below) for any special requirements.

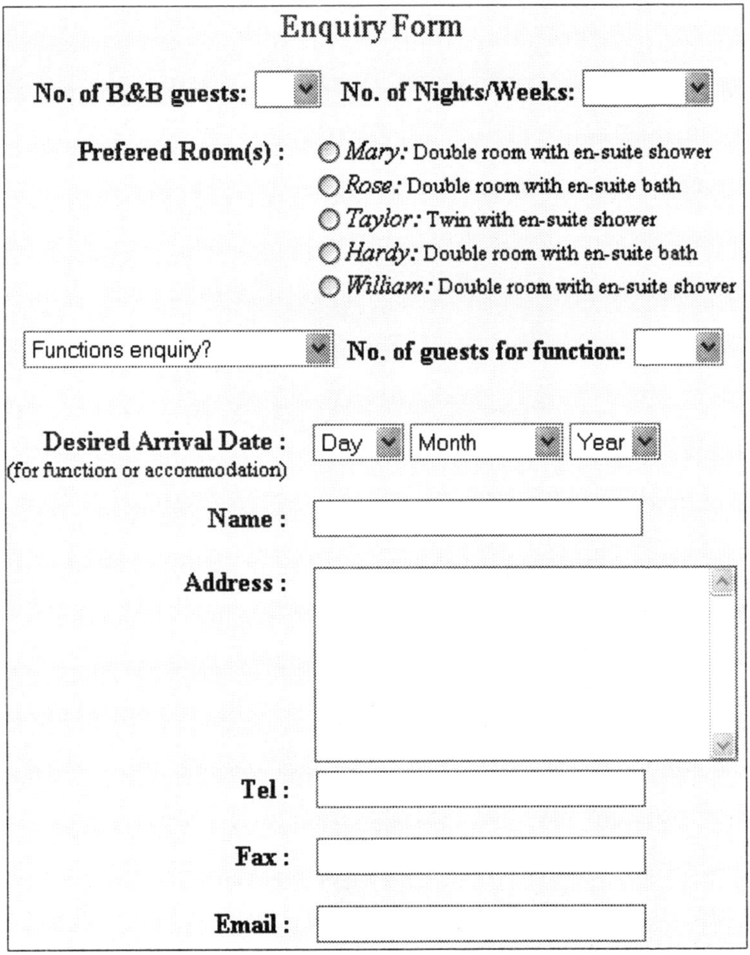

Enquiry Form

No. of B&B guests: [▼]   **No. of Nights/Weeks:** [▼]

Prefered Room(s) :
○ *Mary:* Double room with en-suite shower
○ *Rose:* Double room with en-suite bath
○ *Taylor:* Twin with en-suite shower
○ *Hardy:* Double room with en-suite bath
○ *William:* Double room with en-suite shower

[Functions enquiry?   ▼]   **No. of guests for function:** [▼]

Desired Arrival Date :
(for function or accommodation)
[Day ▼] [Month   ▼] [Year ▼]

Name : [   ]

Address : [   ]

Tel : [   ]

Fax : [   ]

Email : [   ]

Bed and Breakfast Directories

A simple search in Google using the keywords **bed** and **breakfast** will include in the results a number of online directories of guest houses and hotels. If you select **pages from the UK**, when specifying the search criteria in Google, as shown below, most of the establishments in the results list will be in Britain and Ireland; or you can select **the web** to extend the search worldwide. Alternatively, narrow the search down by entering a specific destination such as Amsterdam, as shown below.

Many of the online bed and breakfast directories operate in a similar way. First you select the region in which you want to find accommodation. This might involve clicking a country in a list or on a map of the world. Or it might involve selecting a county in Britain or Ireland. A more detailed map will then be presented allowing you to select your destination precisely.

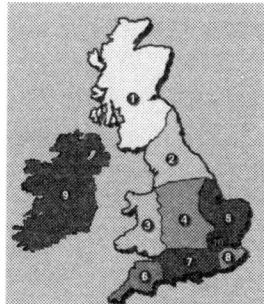

Then the directory will present you with a list of bed and breakfast establishments in your selected area.

When you have viewed the accommodation and found one you like, a booking form can be completed online and e-mailed to the business. Alternatively contact the guest house or hotel directly by e-mail or telephone. The Web addresses of some online bed and breakfast agencies are listed below. To view an agency's Web site, enter the address into the address bar of Internet Explorer.

www.visitus.co.uk

www.accommodata.co.uk

www.bed-breakast-uk.com

www.mybedbreakfast.com

www.bedandbreakfastnationwide.com

www.bedandbreakfasts-uk.co.uk

A Holiday in Venice

The arrival of the low-cost airlines combined with the online facilities of the Internet make it quite feasible to arrange your own accommodation in a city like Venice. There are numerous ways to find accommodation to match your requirements. A search with Google for **venice hotels** produces lots of useful results.

Many of these Web sites are of a very high standard and are worth looking at for their style and artistic qualities alone. For an elegant example, have a look at the Hotel Cipriani, an Orient-Express establishment voted "the world's best hotel". This site gives an excellent pictorial tour of the hotel and also of some of Venice's leading artistic and architectural attractions.

www.hotelcipriani.com

The list of search results also contained a link to the **invenicehotels.com** Web site shown below.

www.invenicehotels.com

This site includes brief descriptions of a large range of hotels in Venice, displayed in various categories such as price, area and star rating.

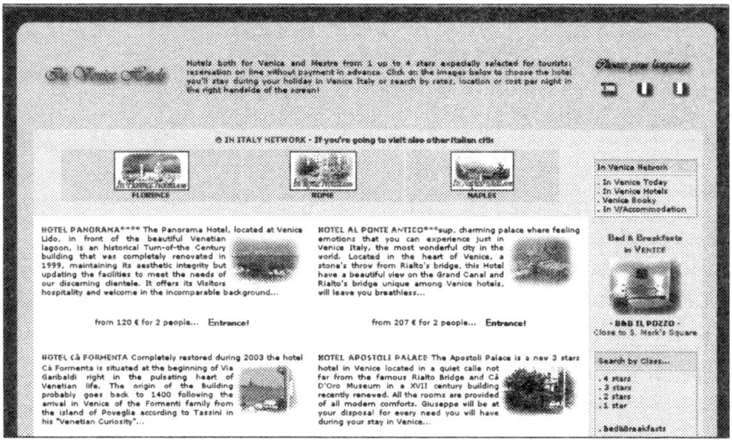

There are links leading to a more detailed page for each hotel, giving details of the accommodation and photographs of the rooms and the surrounding vicinity.

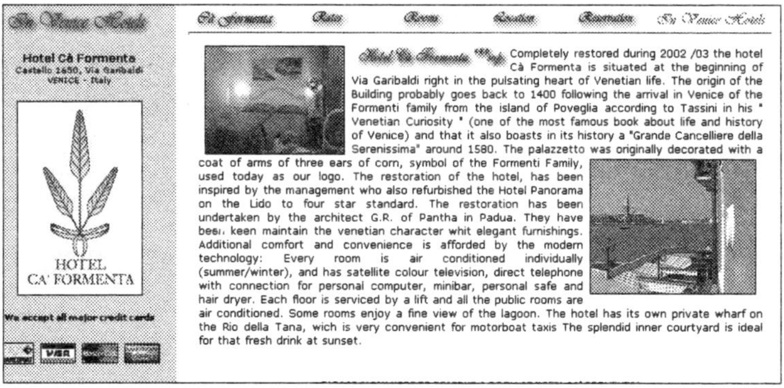

The group of hotels displayed can be selected according to various criteria, such as the number of stars, the rate in euros (usually for two people per night) and the area of Venice. Clicking on one of the links shown below displays a particular group of hotels.

Search by Class...	Search by Rate...	Search by Area...
. 4 stars	. less than 100 €	. San Marco
. 3 stars	. less than 150 €	. San Polo
. 2 stars	. less than 200 €	. Castello
. 1 star	. less than 250 €	. Dorsoduro
		. Cannaregio
. Bed&Breakfasts		. Santa Croce
		. Lido Beach

Having selected a hotel you then complete an online booking form giving the dates of your trip, the number of rooms required and your personal details such as name and address. If the required rooms are available you then make an online booking after supplying your credit card details. (Security of financial transactions over the Internet is discussed in Chapter 10 of this book.)

Many hotel Web sites also display helpful notes and pictures of the top visitor attractions, such as the following from the **invenicehotels.com** site. These include the famous Rialto Bridge and Saint Mark's Basilica, for example.

INTEREST POINTS close to HOTEL AL PONTE ANTICO!

Saint Mark's Basilica: beautiful Venetian church with 5 domes looks like the ancient church of Costantinopoli. It was embellished during the early centuries of the last millennium and particulary in the thirtheenth century when Venice dominated Mediterranean culture and economy. The church, built to represent the power of Serenissima, is externally embellished with marble, mosaics and bas-relief: all maded with precious materials came from Bisanzio, Aquileia and Ravenna. Internally, the church has a Greek cross plan with domes substained by big columns. But the most amazing fact of this church is that the architectural structure is perfectly hidden by the beauty of the mosaics...

Rialto Bridge: TIll thirteenth century Venice was built on a groups of islands separated by channels and to get on the other side were laid down wood boards. Later many bridges were built in Venice but no one of them joining the Gran Canal's banks. This was a big problem for the Establishment so that population was always teasing it about this premise. Competition had been won by **Antonio da Ponte** who thought a unic arch bridge, 48 meters long and 22 meters wide. Foundation was started in 1588, and it took some years to finally join the opposite part of the Gran Canal and subsitute the previous wood bridge that many times collapsed before. To get an image of this previous bridge look at the famous painting by **Carpaccio** "Guarigione di un ossesso")...

Ca'   D'Oro: Once upon the time was considered one of the most sumptuous buildings of Venice for the beautiful colours of its facade. Ca' D'oro knew an unlucky period becouse of the several restorations made during five centuries of history, till baron Giorgio Franchetti bought it at the end of XIX century to create an art gallery. Inside it's possible to admire masterpieces by Mantegna, Diana and Carpaccio. Besides there are many paintings of Flemish school and what remain of the decorations that one time made beautiful the facades of the buildings near the "Canal Grande" (main channel of Venice).

All of the major online travel companies such as **expedia.co.uk**, **travelocity.co.uk**, **ebookers.com**, **onlinetravel.com**, **mytravel.com**, **thisistravel.co.uk** and **cheapflights.co.uk** have links to hotel booking sites.

The **cheapaccommodation.com** site shown below is accessed by clicking a hotels link off the **cheapflights.co.uk** Web site.

www.cheapflights.co.uk

www.cheapaccommodation.com

From this site you can look for accommodation in all of the major cities of the world; you can choose between hotels with different star ratings (from 1 to 5), or look for hostels, villas and apartments. Then, having checked details such as room availability and price, you can make an online booking.

The next chapter looks at the use of the Internet to help with travel documents, legal and medical issues and last-minute preparations before setting off.

9

Last Minute Preparations

Introduction

When you've booked the accommodation and arranged your transport, there are still quite a lot of smaller tasks to be done before you are ready for the trip. Many of these tasks are extremely important and need to be carried out conscientiously if potential disasters are to be avoided. Obviously the preparations are simpler if you're taking a trip in your own country, since you won't need to worry about passports, visas or inoculations, etc.

This chapter looks at the way the Internet can be used to help with the final preparations for your travel and holidays, under the following headings:

- Holiday checklists.
- Passports, visas, embassies and consulates, etc.
- Foreign currency, travellers cheques, credit cards.
- Medical matters.
- Travel Insurance.
- Consumer protection, ATOL and ABTA.

Holiday Checklists

Most of us have probably scribbled out lists of tasks to do before going on holiday - cancel the milk and newspapers, book the dog into the kennels, etc. However, there are now lots of Web sites which have taken checklists to new levels of sophistication. **Don't Forget Your Toothbrush** is a Web site providing hundreds of checklist tasks which can be tailored to your particular trip, such as a summer holiday, driving in Europe, camping and caravanning or winter skiing. Tasks are prioritised according to the amount of time needed - for example, obtaining a new passport or arranging vaccinations might take several weeks. The personalized checklist can be printed out then completed by ticking the boxes. To see the complete Web site enter the following into the address bar of the Internet Explorer.

www.dontforgetyourtoothbrush.com/uk/howitworks.asp

Planning Ahead

The first step to creating the ultimate holiday checklist is to plan ahead. F our comprehensive planning lists, tick the items that you would like to ad your personal list.

It might be argued that you don't need the Internet to produce a holiday checklist. However, a quick Google search for keywords like **holiday checklists**, for example, provides a number of checklists with some useful tips which some of us might not be aware of, such as:

- The Royal Mail Keepsafe service will hold your mail for up to 2 months, for a small charge.

- Do you already make photocopies of all of your important travel documents and place copies in the hotel safe?

These documents might include your passport, visa, E111 form and any medical prescriptions (including a prescription for your glasses, if necessary). The Foreign and Commonwealth Office Web site displays free checklists and advice for anyone travelling abroad.

www.fco.gov.uk

© Crown Copyright

The online checklists may also have links to travel insurance web sites. The checklists stress the need to check that the policy covers all of your insurance requirements, as shown below in an extract from the **BEFORE YOU GO** section of the Foreign and Commonwealth Office Website, discussed on the previous page.

Checklist

Travel Advice

Check the Foreign & Commonwealth Office (FCO)Travel Advice, or contact the FCO on 0870 606 0290.

Get adequate travel insurance.

- Make sure it includes comprehensive medical and repatriation cover.
- Make sure it provides cover for your whole trip (whether one day or over a year).
- Make sure it covers you for all activities, including hazardous sports.
- Disclose pre-existing medical conditions.
- Take your policy number and the 24-hour emergency number with you.
- If you have any doubts about your cover, check with your insurer.

Ensure you have a valid passport and the necessary visas.

- Make sure your passport is valid for a minimum of six months at return date.
- Take a photocopy with you and leave a copy at home.
- Write the full details of your next of kin in your passport.
- Make sure you have valid visas.
- Take another form of ID with you (preferably with a photograph).

If the very worst should happen, travel insurance should provide an air ambulance to fly you home, if necessary.

Most of us would realize that we need to check our driving licence and car insurance before driving abroad. However, the Green Card normally provided only gives minimal third-party cover - an extra payment may be needed to ensure comprehensive cover. For driving in Spain, you are advised to purchase a "Bail Bond" to enable you and your car to be released after an accident.

The holiday checklists on the Internet are useful both for the basic "packing" tasks to be completed before going away but also for the links they provide to other sites.

Many of the checklists have a link to the Foreign and Commonwealth Office Web site, discussed previously, where you can read the latest information and advice about travelling to countries where safety or health may be issues.

www.fco.gov.uk

Some of the Web sites have checklists with links to sites providing insurance and foreign currency. There is also advice on the use of credit cards abroad and links to sites showing the location of cash machines in foreign cities.

There may also be a link to the Web site of the UK Passport Office where you can apply for a passport online and find out about requirements in certain countries. Examples of Web sites including holiday checklists are as follows:

www.ebookers.com

(Select **Travel with care** under **Travel Tools**).

www.virgin.net/travel/features/checklist.html

www.dontforgetyourtoothbrush.com

www.tescofinance.com/personal/finance

(Select **Smarter money** and **Going on holiday**).

www.bbc.co.uk/holiday/traveltools/checklist.shtml

www.heathrow-airport-hotels-online.co.uk/checklists.htm

Passports and Visas

Your passport will be checked on entry to most countries overseas and some will also require a visa. Even when travelling on domestic flights within the UK it's a good idea to carry your passport as a form of identification.

You can apply for a passport online or renew or amend an existing one, at the Web site of the United Kingdom Passport Service (UKPS).

www.ukpa.gov.uk

After you fill in your details online, an application form is printed out by the passport office and returned to you by conventional post, for you to sign, date and enclose the relevant photographs and documents before returning.

A visa may involve stamping the passport or attaching a sticker and allows entry to a country for a limited time. The need for a visa depends on your nationality, destination and the duration of your stay in a country. The Foreign and Commonwealth Office Web site contains advice about passport and visa requirements in different countries.

www.fco.gov.uk

© Crown Copyright

The Foreign and Commonwealth Office Web site contains a list of contact details for foreign consulates and embassies based in this country. You should contact the London-based consulate or embassy of the country you are visiting for the latest visa requirements (and any other travel advice, such as dangers, conflicts, or health issues).

The Foreign and Commonwealth Office Web site contains a list of helpful tips relating to looking after your passport and what to do if you lose it while abroad.

There are also lists of Travellers Tips for different countries; for example penalties for certain offences may be much harsher than for the same offence in the United Kingdom. To read the travel advice for a particular country, you click the country's name listed under **TRAVEL ADVICE**, as shown below.

© Crown Copyright

The Foreign and Commonwealth Office Web site is located at:

www.fco.gov.uk

UK Embassies Overseas

The Foreign and Commonwealth Office Web site also has a link to a list of British Embassies, High Commissions and Consulates overseas. Before leaving home, note the address(es) in the countries you are visiting, for example the British Honorary Consul in Venice, shown below.

© Crown Copyright

The Embassy or Consulate staff should be able to help if you have a genuine problem, such as losing your passport. Should you have the misfortune to need legal services while abroad on holiday, the Foreign and Commonwealth Office Web site also contains lists of English-speaking lawyers in countries overseas.

Travel Money

Try typing something like **travel currency** as keywords in Google and you will find lots of sites giving exchange rates and currency converters. Many of the sites also give sound general advice such as taking your money in a mixture of formats - some notes and coins for immediate expenses, some travellers cheques and also credit or debit cards.

Some banks and other organizations allow you to order currency online, for postal delivery the next day, with a typical delivery charge of £5.

There are lots of currency converters on the Internet, such as the one shown below on the ebookers.com Web site.

You can select 3 different foreign currencies plus travellers cheques, then enter the amount of Sterling (£) and select small, mixed or large denominations of the currency notes.

After clicking **Continue,** the amounts of foreign currency are calculated, together with buy-back details, any commission and arrangements for collecting the currency.

Credit and Debit Cards

Mastercard and Visa cards can be used in thousands of cash machines around the world. Your bank's Web site will probably have an online cash machine locator or you can visit the Mastercard or Visa sites. For example, the Visa cash machine locator is shown below. First you select the region and the country off a map of the world.

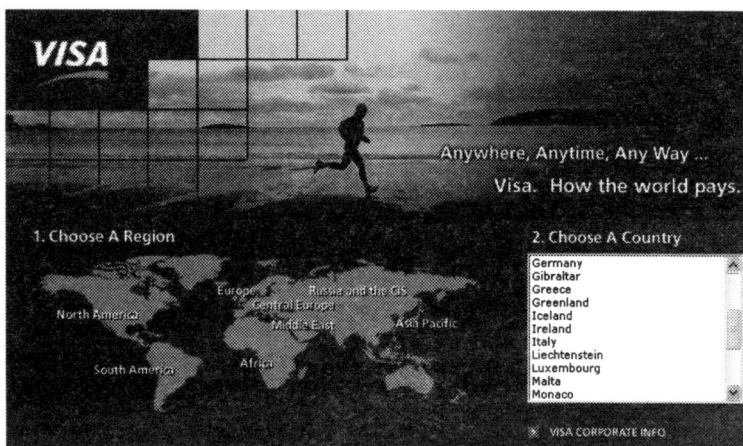

After selecting **Find a cash machine** and entering the name of the city, a map showing the location of the machines appears, together with a listing of their addresses.

In the example shown on the next page, Visa machines in Venice were found. A total of 41 cash machines are located in the city and these are displayed in groups of 5.

Relevant Web sites

www.visa.com

www.mastercard.com

www.thisismoney.com

At the top of the Web page shown above there is a button marked **I've lost my Visa**. Click this button for advice and menus giving you emergency numbers to ring (24 hours a day) to report lost cards or lost travellers cheques. Before travelling, also consult the Web site of your high-street bank and make a note of all emergency telephone numbers.

Medical Matters

If a medical crisis occurs, your travel insurance should cover the cost of treatment while you're abroad and the cost of flying you home by air ambulance. However, there are a number of steps you can take to reduce the risk of serious health problems. These are described in the health section of the **KNOW BEFORE YOU GO** campaign on the Foreign and Commonwealth Office Web site shown below.

© Crown Copyright

Apart from general advice, such as checking what vaccinations are needed at least six weeks before you go, and packing your medication in your hand luggage, there is a link to a page outlining the cover and limitations of the E111 form. This is a form obtainable from the post office and entitling you to free or reduced cost state health cover in European countries. E111 does not replace travel insurance, which is still essential.

www.fco.gov.uk

On the right of the **BEFORE YOU GO** page on the Foreign and Commonwealth Office Web site shown on the previous page is a series of links to other Web pages. For example, **Long Distance Travel** gives tips for avoiding dehydration and circulation problems such as deep vein thrombosis. There is also advice on special steps to take if you are suffering from asthma, diabetes or any from of disability.

In the section **Advice for Other Travellers**, a link entitled **Older Travellers** presents the following advice.

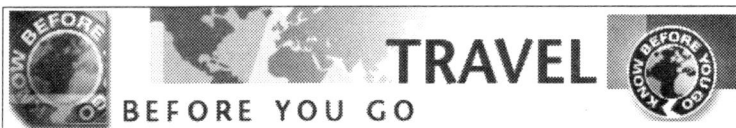

Older Travellers

Many older people travel overseas to visit relatives or to fulfil long-standing tourist ambitions. Good preparation can prevent many potential health problems and make a holiday much more enjoyable.

Tips:

- Always declare existing health problems – including any arranged hospital admissions – when buying travel insurance.
- Check with your doctor about where you are going and how. Ask him about vaccinations and anti-malarial medication.
- A pre-travel health consultation may reveal the need for special advice on the mode of travel, choice of destinations and route.
- Ask your doctor for adequate medication for the whole trip and any delays.
- Lack of exercise in airports and on aircraft can result in venous thrombosis and possibly pulmonary embolism (blood clots in the lungs). Ask the cabin crew about simple exercises you can do on flights.
- Angina and breathlessness can be worse at high altitude and sometimes in aircraft. If warned in advance the airlines can provide additional oxygen.
- Avoid getting mosquito bites by using mosquito nets, covering up and using mosquito repellents. Check with your doctor about what anti-malarial medication to take.

© Crown Copyright

Travel Insurance

If you have arranged your holiday as part of a package, travel insurance may be included. However, you may wish to arrange your own cover through the Internet or through an agency such as the Post Office. Travel insurance is also included free with certain bank accounts and credit cards. There may be a discount for buying online.

If you suffer from any pre-existing medical condition, this should be declared immediately. If not, you may find a subsequent claim being refused. If you have trouble finding travel insurance, have a look at the Age Concern Web site, which includes a link to **Age Concern Travel Insurance**, (under **Products & Services**), which has no upper age limits and also includes **Annual Multi-trip Travel Insurance**.

www.ageconcern.org.uk

Most travel insurance Web sites advise that you should make sure that your policy covers:

- All medical expenses, including an air ambulance to fly you home and also repatriating your family.
- Personal Liability
- Personal Accident
- Cancellation and curtailment
- Personal baggage
- Legal Expenses

The Seniors Network has a helpful section on travel insurance, including companies which provide cover for older people at reasonable prices. There are also several reports from older travellers recounting their experiences of obtaining travel insurance from different companies.

www.seniorsnetwork.co.uk

Consumer Protection

There are several schemes and organisations which regulate travel companies and protect customers.

ATOL – The Air Travel Organisers' Licence

ATOL is managed by the Civil Aviation Authority (CAA) and protects customers who buy flights and holidays *through a licensed travel agent* in the UK. Travel companies are required to deposit bonds with the CAA; if a company fails, the CAA refunds the customer (if they have not yet started their holiday) or alternatively arranges for them to continue a holiday and fly home.

Web sites of travel companies with an ATOL licence should display the logo shown on the right. You can check the licence after entering the ATOL Web site using the address given below.

www.atol.org.uk

Check with your travel agent that your trip is ATOL protected. If you book a flight directly with an airline, rather than through a licensed travel agent, the flight will not be ATOL protected.

ABTA – The Association of British Travel Agents

Travel agents and tour operators in the United Kingdom who are members of ABTA place a bond with the association. This enables customers to continue their holiday if a company fails, or provides a full refund. ABTA companies are also required to maintain high standards of quality and to ensure that holiday descriptions are accurate. Member companies display the ABTA logo shown on the right on their Web pages.

The ABTA Web site shown below has a comprehensive range of consumer services including assistance with complaints against ABTA companies, independent arbitration for complaints and disability issues.

www.abta.com

The Association of British Travel Agents

about ABTA   Research your trip   How to use ABTAnet to   Consumer Services   Members Area

flights   offers   jobs

Who goes where?
Find ABTA member companies featuring

as a destination for their holidays

This **ABTAnet** e-directory includes details of ABTA's 2300 members - UK travel agents and tour operators - with information on the destinations they feature and their special skills.

Claiming for Holiday Disasters

This is Money is a financial Web site giving, amongst many other things, advice on how to claim for all sorts of holiday disasters such as false descriptions, over-booking and incomplete building works. Enter the Web address shown below into the address bar in Internet Explorer, then do a site search for **disasters**.

www.thisismoney.com

Security of Online Transactions

Introduction

It's natural to be concerned about paying for travel and holidays over the Internet, by entering credit card details. Even though this method of purchase may give a healthy discount and can be carried out from the comfort of your own home, you are bound to worry if you are spending hundreds or thousands of pounds on a holiday. Credit cards are a modern phenomenon and many older people are more comfortable with transactions using cash or cheques.

However, online financial transactions are actually very safe, provided you follow some commonsense precautions outlined shortly. Making purchases over the Internet is certainly less risky than allowing your credit card to disappear into the back of a restaurant, for example, where it could be copied or "skimmed" using a special device.

Many of the large banks and other companies are so confident of online security that they guarantee that no customer will lose money as a result of online trading. Several online businesses have stated that none of their customers has reported fraudulent use of a credit or debit card as a result of online purchases made with them.

Precautions Taken by Online Businesses

Secure Servers

Servers are the computers used by banks and online companies to hold the details of millions of transactions and customers' accounts. *Secure servers* use *encryption,* which scrambles or encodes the information travelling between customers' computers and the online business. The information can only be decoded, i.e. made intelligible, by authorized users. The chances of a hacker unscrambling the information are negligible.

Organisations such as banks and large companies use an encryption level known as *128-bit SSL (Secure Sockets Layer).* Whenever you are online to a secure server, a small closed padlock icon appears at the bottom right of your screen. Double-click the padlock icon to reveal details of the security certificate issued to the company. Always deal with companies who use secure servers. Secure Web pages also have an address starting **https://** rather than simply **http://**.

Warnings of E-mail Scams

Please note that although encryption prevents your personal and financial details entering the wrong hands, during transactions involving secure servers, it is not possible to encrypt data sent in e-mails. In recent "scams" bank customers were asked to supply personal financial details by e-mail, in messages purporting to have been sent by the banks. These e-mails can appear genuine and you need to be very vigilant to spot them. The banks have therefore sent out warnings that they never ask for customers' details by e-mail. Never send your financial details in an e-mail.

Defeating Trojans

Some customers have received e-mails, claiming to be from their bank, which contained an attached file known as a Trojan. A Trojan is a malicious program which often masquerades as something quite innocent. The Trojan can record the keys that have been pressed, such as a password or memorable word and then relay the information back to the "hacker's" own computer.

When logging onto your online account, banks often require you to enter a few letters from a memorable word. To defeat the Trojan, you must select the letters with a mouse from a drop-down menu, rather than typing using the keyboard. Another defence against the Trojan is to install up-to-date anti-virus software, provided free by some banks. Anti-virus software is discussed shortly.

Cookies

Web sites which you visit send back information about you and store it on your own computer as a small text file, known as a "cookie". A cookie records your preferences and interests. This simplifies your next visit to the Web site. Banking information may be stored in *session cookies*; for security these cookies are deleted as soon as you log off. Next time you log on the whole log-in process must be repeated, to prevent unauthorized access. Cookies are also used by Web site owners to gather statistics and marketing information.

You can set the way your computer responds to cookies by selecting **Tools**, **Internet Options...**, and **Privacy** in Internet Explorer. You can prevent a site from sending you cookies but some Web sites cannot be accessed unless your computer is set to receive the cookies.

Keeping Your Financial Transactions Safe

If you pay for goods and services over the Internet, a *credit card* gives the most security, since the card company may (if there has been no fraud or negligence) refund all purchases over £100, if the goods or services are unsatisfactory or not delivered on time. (A debit card, like cash, doesn't offer the same protection). However, you should still make every effort to prevent fraud and breaches of security. The following advice is given by banks and other organizations for online financial transactions in general, but applies equally to travel and holiday online bookings.

- Don't write down your card, account or pin numbers or leave them lying around on bits of paper, or store them on your computer.

- Choose obscure passwords and memorable words and don't write them down. Don't use pets' names, family names or birthdays, etc.

- Don't allow anyone to look over your shoulder while entering passwords, account numbers, etc.

- Change passwords and memorable words regularly.

- Only make online transactions with companies displaying a street address, telephone number, etc. Whenever possible choose well-known companies.

- Make sure that the Web pages involved in the actual payment (where you enter your credit card details) display a *closed* padlock, denoting a secure server. A secure server may also be represented by a key which is *solid* rather than cracked. Also look for **https://** rather than simply **http://** in the **Web** address.

- Double-click the icon for the padlock or key to check the security certificate. It should give the name of the company and the dates for which the certificate is valid.

- Monitor your monthly credit card statements and make sure you can account for each transaction. Inform your credit card supplier immediately if you are suspicious of a transaction or a supplier of goods or services.

- If you intend to spend heavily on your credit card while on holiday, inform your credit card company. Otherwise their routine checks may detect this as an unusual pattern of spending and put a block on the card - extremely inconvenient if you're abroad on holiday at the time.

- Make printouts of any online booking forms so that you have a copy of all the relevant details, including prices, dates, etc. Destroy any reference to your account numbers, card numbers, etc. (The printing of Web pages is discussed in Chapter 4, Capturing Travel and Holiday Web Pages).

- Never include your credit card details in an e-mail. No card company will ever ask you, unsolicited, for your card information or PINs, by e-mail or via a Web site.

- Always log out of a financial Web site as soon as you've finished your transaction - don't walk away and leave the computer still connected to the site.

- Be especially careful if using an Internet connection in a public place such as an office, library or Internet café.

Protecting Your Computer

There are three main methods of protecting your computer on the Internet from people of malicious or criminal intent. Protection involves installing the following software:

- An effective anti-virus program.
- An Internet firewall.
- Regular updates to Microsoft Windows.

These software installations are not very costly and can save hours of inconvenience and possible expense. If you don't feel like installing the software yourself, a small local computer business should do the work in a matter of minutes. Symantec sells the Norton range of anti-virus and security software products and includes a free security audit of your computer. Log on to the Web site shown below and select the **Security Check** button.

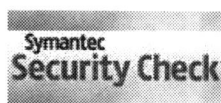

www.symantec.com

Security Status: Safe!
You are protected against most common security threats.

 = At Risk!   = Possible Risk! = Safe

Hacker Exposure Check

Windows Vulnerability Check

Trojan Horse Check

Antivirus Product Check

Virus Protection Update Check

The Threat of Viruses

A virus is a small computer program written maliciously to damage software and data and to cause inconvenience to the user. Unfortunately the files on your hard disc are vulnerable to attack from computer viruses, unless you take precautions to protect them. This means installing some anti-virus software and keeping it up to date so that the program recognizes the latest viruses.

The virus enters a computer system insidiously, often from a rogue floppy disc or an e-mail. If not detected the virus multiplies and spreads throughout a hard disc. Some viruses may only cause trivial damage - such as displaying a so-called 'humorous' message - while others, such as **"Ripper"** or **"Jack the Ripper"**, shown below, can destroy files or wipe an entire hard disc.

Virus Information

Virus Name:	Ripper
Aliases:	Jack the Ripper
Infects:	Floppy and Master Boot Records
Likelihood:	Common
Length:	520 bytes

Characteristics

✔ Memory Resident   ⊘ Triggered Event

⊘ Size Stealth   ⊘ Encrypting

✔ Full Stealth   ⊘ Polymorphic

Comments

When active in memory, Ripper will randomly corrupt disk writes. App every 1,000 disk writes will be affected. The virus contains the encr

Even when a virus doesn't do any serious damage to files and software, getting rid of it may waste a lot of valuable time - not to mention the anxiety caused if you fear the loss of files which may be very important to you.

Writing viruses is an act of vandalism and can result in a prison sentence. Viruses can exist on floppy and hard discs. They can also reside temporarily in the computer's memory - but they are removed from the memory when the computer is switched off. Viruses do not permanently damage the physical parts of a computer, i.e. hardware components such as the memory or the printer.

Viruses can also enter your system from the Internet, perhaps through e-mail *attachments*, the programs or documents "clipped" onto an e-mail.

The Norton AntiVirus software package has a scanning program (called Auto-Protect) which constantly monitors e-mail attachments being downloaded to your computer from an Internet mail server.

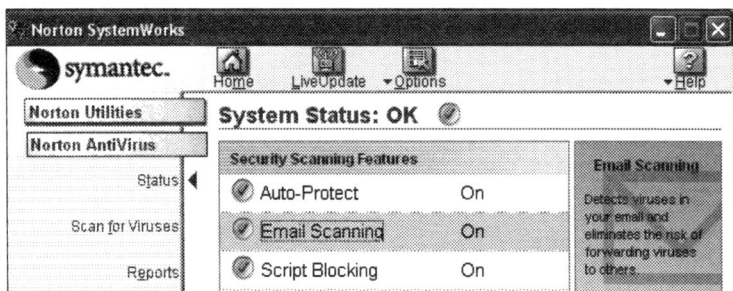

Great care should be taken when opening e-mails of doubtful origin; if you are suspicious the e-mail should be deleted immediately without opening.

Anti-Virus Software

Recent years have seen the evolution of an ever-increasing list of computer viruses. Several major companies have developed anti-virus software to detect and eradicate virus infection. Three of the leading software packages are Norton AntiVirus, McAfee VirusScan, and F-Secure. There are currently nearly 70,000 computer viruses, each with their own name such as MyDoom, Netsky and Blaster, presently much in evidence. *Worms* are viruses which can spread around networks including the Internet.

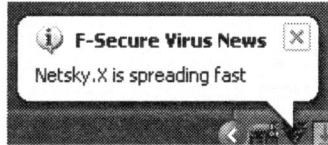

F-Secure Virus News

April 20, 2004	Virus News: Netsky.X is spreading fast
April 12, 2004	Virus News: The Macintosh MP3 trojan case
April 4, 2004	Virus News: Sober.F spreading in Europe
March 29, 2004	Virus News: Netsky.Q autoexecutes itself

Many viruses enter the computer as attachments or files clipped to e-mails. Never open e-mail attachments unless you are absolutely certain of the e-mail's origin.

Anti-virus software installed on your computer should detect any viruses and delete them before they can do any damage. Since new viruses are being invented all the time, your anti-virus software needs to be updated regularly by downloading information to enable it to recognize and deal with the latest viruses. Some anti-virus programs are updated automatically while you are online to the Internet.

Some of the functions of anti-virus software are:

- To continually monitor the memory and vulnerable files, to prevent viruses entering the hard disc and spreading, causing havoc and destruction. **The Real-time Protection** feature in F-Secure ensures that all files are scanned whenever they are accessed.

- To allow the user to carry out *manual scans* to check the memory, floppy and hard discs, whenever it is felt necessary.

- To remove viruses by repairing or deleting files.

- To provide a list of definitions of known viruses, which is regularly updated via the Internet.

- To schedule regular scans at certain times, as shown below in the screenshot from F-Secure.

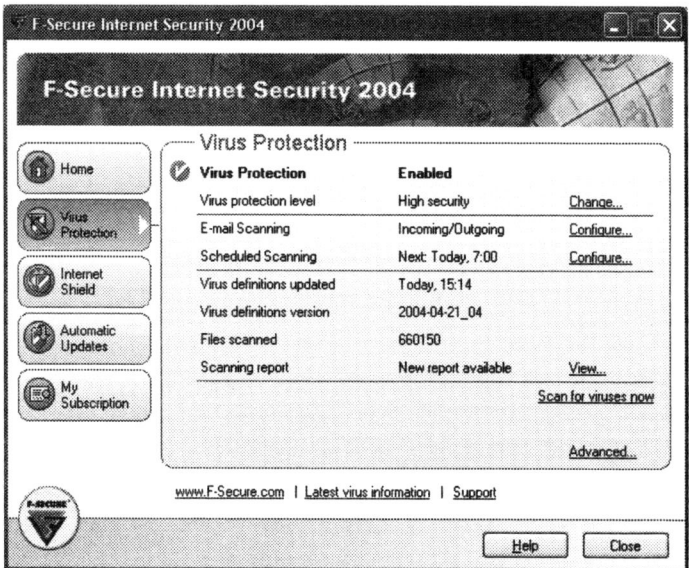

Internet Firewalls

A *firewall* is a piece of software designed to stop "hackers" or malicious people from gaining access to your computer from across the Internet. In the worst case it might be possible for a hacker to connect to your computer and find out credit card and other financial information. The firewall detects other computers trying to connect to yours and either blocks them if they appear suspicious or lets you decide whether to allow or refuse access.

Windows XP has a built-in Internet firewall and there are numerous third-party firewall software packages from companies such as Norton, Sygate, eTrust EZ and McAfee. Some integrated software packages, such as F-Secure Internet Security 2004, include a built-in firewall, known as the **Internet Shield**, as well as **Virus Protection** and **Automatic Updates** to the list of virus definitions.

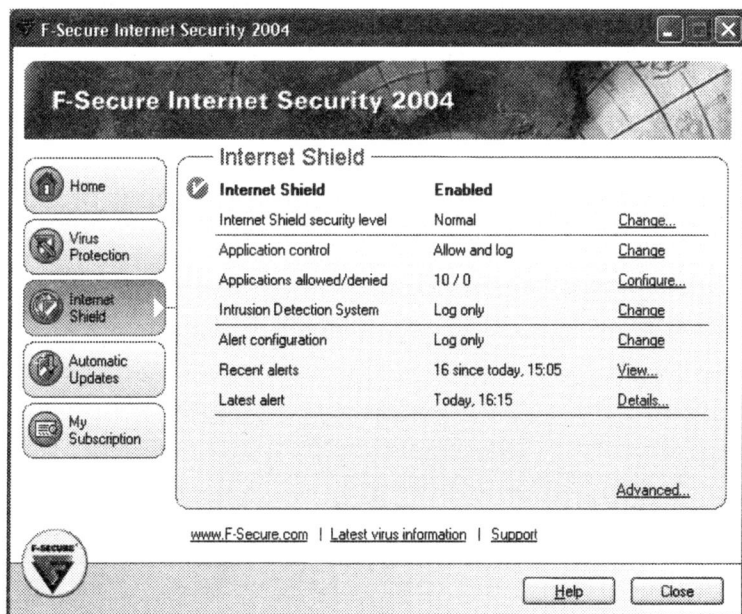

Updates to Microsoft Windows

The dominance of the Microsoft Windows operating system has made hackers even more determined to find security weaknesses which can be exploited. In response, Microsoft regularly issues "patches" or repairs to the software. These patches can be downloaded from the Internet using a feature called Microsoft Windows Update. The system examines your computer and tells you which of the software updates need to be installed.

Critical Updates and Service Packs

Critical updates are already selected for you to install
Review the list of critical updates below. You can remove any item you don't want.

Review and install updates   Total items selected: (1)

Security Update for Windows XP (KB828028)
Download size: 311 KB
A security issue has been identified in Microsoft Windows-based systems that could allow an attacker to compromise your Microsoft Windows-based system and gain control over it. You can help protect your computer by installing this update from Microsoft. After you install this item, you may need to restart your computer. Read more...

This item has been selected.   Add   Remove

You can switch on automatic updates in Windows XP by clicking **start** and **Control Panel**. Now double-click the **System** icon shown on the right. (If you can't see the **System** icon, click **Switch to Classic** view on the top left of the **Control Panel**.)

System

Control Panel

Switch to Classic View

The system properties dialogue box is displayed, from which you select the **Automatic Updates** tab. There are various options for installing the updates to Windows, which you select by clicking on one of the 3 radio buttons shown below. These include scheduling the updates to Windows to be installed automatically on a regular day and a time which you specify, as shown below. Or you can choose to be notified of necessary updates and decide when you want to install them on your computer.

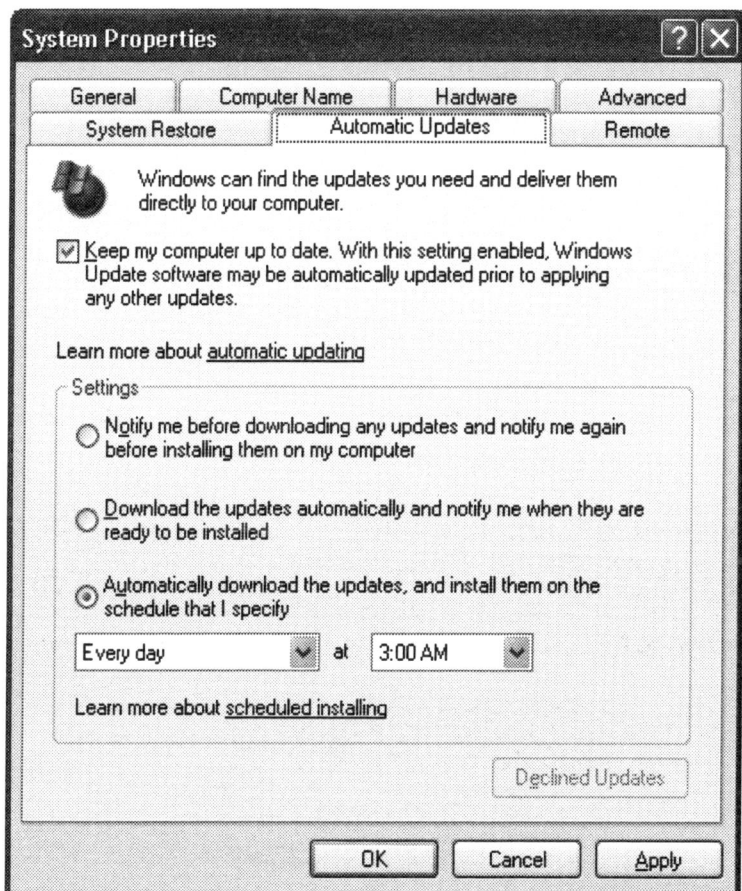

10 Security of Online Transactions

Appendix:
Sites of Special Interest to Older Travellers

The following Web sites are either devoted exclusively to the over-50s, etc., or they have sections within them which are pertinent. Also listed are Web sites catering for travellers with special needs. (The Web addresses of many of the large travel and holiday companies are given in the relevant sections in this book).

To view each Web site, enter the address into the **Address** bar in Internet Explorer, as shown below. (You don't need to type the **http://** part, just the bit starting **www.**, etc.)

www.seniorsnetwork.co.uk

This site has lots of advice about holidays, travel and travel insurance, with links to many of the big travel and holiday Web sites (plus many other topics to interest older people).

www.travel-quest.co.uk

Specialist travel and holidays are listed here, including a section for seniors and silver surfers. All sorts of holidays in the UK and around the world are listed, to suit every taste, including adventures and special interests.

www.travel55.co.uk

A specialist travel Web site for the over-50s, with links to all types of holiday, hotels, coach, villas, short breaks, self-catering, cruising, golfing, singles, etc. Also links to flights, ferries and trains. This is a sister site to the CenNet over-50s lifestyle site and gives 5 to 10% discounts with participating travel and holiday companies.

www.saga.co.uk

The long-established holiday site for the over-50s provides package holidays in the UK, Europe and all over the world including cruises aboard the Saga Rose and Saga Pearl.

www.cennet.co.uk

The CenNet site is a general lifestyle site for the over-50s and includes a travel section with links to all sorts of holidays all over the world, including singles, golfing, self-catering, cruises, plus online booking of ferries, trains, flights, car hire and travel insurance.

www.responsibletravel.com

Worldwide holidays for the over-50s with the emphasis on conservation and benefits to the local community, while respecting local cultures and religions. Includes over-50s adventure holidays, culture, walking and hiking and safaris.

www.thebestis-yet.com

The Best is Yet to Come site is a guide to retirement or 'Life after work', with the emphasis on humour and also keeping fit. Lots of holidays cottages are listed in the UK and links to a variety of holidays in the UK and abroad. There is also a message board where you can chat to others about anything you like, including travel and holidays.

www.laterlife.co.uk

This is a complete lifestyle guide for the over-50s and includes a travel section edited by a veteran travel guide and tour manager. Includes a comprehensive guide to worldwide holidays suitable for the over-50s. There is also a section on long-stay winter holidays, which, it is said, can prove cheaper than stopping at home.

www.50plusexpeditions.com

These are adventure holidays designed for the over-50s. Expeditions consist of small groups experiencing new activities such as rafting on a jungle river, riding an elephant, or cruising in a small ship. Walking activities can range from easy to demanding.

www.silversurfers.net

This site covers all aspects of life for the over-50s, with a comprehensive travel and holiday section giving links to all of the major travel companies. There is a link to a holiday directory for the disabled. Another link takes you to the HomeLink site where you can arrange a holiday involving exchanging houses with a person or family in any one of 50 participating countries.

uk.dir.yahoo.com

This is the Yahoo! Directory. After entering the above address (there is no **www.**) into the address bar you need to navigate through the sub-directories as shown below.

Tour Operators > Seniors
Directory > Business and Economy > Shopping and Services > Travel and Transportation > Tour Operators > **Seniors**

Once on the **Seniors** page there are lots of links to Web sites specializing in 50-plus travel and holidays.

www.find-uk.com

Typing something like **travel insurance senior citizens** into the on-site **Find** bar brings up a list of links to insurance companies offering cover for the older traveller.

www.allsitestravel.co.uk

Click the link **Disabled Travel** on the **allsitestravel** home page to display a list of specialist tour operators catering for the disabled and those with special needs. These include wheelchair-accessible properties and activities such as skiing and African safaris for the disabled.

www.access-travel.co.uk

This site lists holidays for the disabled, including wheelchair-accessible properties, information and facilities such as adapted vehicles and hire of specialist equipment.

www.abletogo.biz

This is a "one-stop" travel and lifestyle Web site offering holidays and hotels for older people and those with mobility problems. This site also offers articles on UK heritage and culture and notes on holidays in Europe and worldwide, with currency delivered to your door and discounts on hotels and flights.

allgohere.com   www.everybody.co.uk

These two related sites, usually known as All Go Here, provide listings of airlines and hotels catering for both disabled and able-bodied travellers. The site details the provision made by airlines for disabled passengers. UK Hotels are rated in 3 categories according to the "Tourism For All" national accessible accommodation standard.

Index